THE WEB PAGE WORKBOOK

Dawn Groves
Bellingham Technical College
Whatcom Community College

Franklin, Beedle & Associates Incorporated
8536 SW St. Helens Drive
Wilsonville, OR 97070
(503) 682-7668
http://www.fbeedle.com

President and Publisher	Jim Leisy (jimleisy@fbeedle.com)
Editor	Samantha Soma
Manuscript Editor	Elizabeth von Radics
Interior Design and Production	Tom Sumner
	Steve Klinetobe
	Karen Foley
Cover Design	Steve Klinetobe
Proofreader	Bill DeRouchey
Marketing Group	Victor Kaiser
	Eric Machado
	Sue Page
	Laura Rowe
Order Processing	Chris Alarid
	Ann Leisy
Manufacturing	Malloy Lithographing
	Ann Arbor, Michigan

Rights and Permissions
FRANKLIN, BEEDLE & ASSOCIATES INCORPORATED
8536 SW St. Helens Drive, Suite D
Wilsonville, Oregon 97070
www.fbeedle.com

Library of Congress Cataloging-in-Publication Data

Groves, Dawn
    The Web page workbook / by Dawn Groves.
       p.   cm.
    Includes index.
    ISBN 1-887902-05-8 (pbk.)
    1. HTML (Document markup language) 2. World Wide Web (Information retrieval system) I. Title.
QA.76.H94G75 1996
005.75--dc20   96-5547
                               CIP

PREFACE

The Web Page Workbook is a text for Web enthusiasts who would like to create useful, appealing Web site presentations quickly and easily. In an easy-to-understand, no-nonsense manner, the book teaches basic HTML and distills volumes of Web design advice and guidance into simple articles and quick-reference lists. Helpful ideas regarding effective Web page promotion are also included. A Web Site Prototype Development Form helps direct your design efforts to facilitate quick results.

If used in a classroom, this book is written to fill four to eight hours of class time, depending on how much of the HTML tutorial is used. All Web page development is completed locally using the Netscape Navigator browser to view and check results. The extensive appendices in the back of the book include resources for HTML study, tag definitions, a character entity table, and additional advice and information regarding Web site development.

- ◎ **Book Organization.** The first half of the book is an HTML tutorial containing minimal narrative and a variety of interesting exercises. It is designed to help you understand and apply the basics of HTML without wasting a lot of time. If possible, you should perform the practice exercises in the sequence dictated by the book.

  The second half of the book includes practical Web design advice and guidance. A Web Site Development Form is included to help direct your efforts and facilitate quick results. Online resources are also listed, as are suggestions for promoting your Web site and attracting visitors to it.

- ◎ **Software.** *The Web Page Workbook* comes bundled with HotDog, a highly rated HTML editor, and Netscape Navigator, arguably the most popular browser on the Web. Because the programs are zipped, PKUNZIP is also included with the diskettes. You will need to install these programs on your hard drive before beginning the tutorial. Simple installation instructions come with the diskettes.

- ◎ **Appendices.** The detailed appendices at the end of the book provide ample reference information. They include an HTML tag table, a list of character entities, advice on improving your HTML skills, a glossary, and an index.

REQUIREMENTS

As an HTML reference, this book can be used by both Macintosh and PC owners. However, the diskettes and their referenced files are formatted for use on a PC.

This book assumes you are familiar with the basic operation of a computer and have at least rudimentary word-processing skills. You should also know how to use the mouse and navigate in a Windows 3.1 or Windows 95 environment. The following hardware requirements should be considered:

1. A personal computer (PC) running Windows 3.1 or Windows 95 with a 386, 486, or Pentium processor.
2. A hard disk with at least 10 megabytes free space for Netscape and HotDog.
3. A bare minimum of four megabytes of RAM; eight megabytes is recommended.
4. A floppy disk drive.
5. A Windows-compatible mouse.

Refer to Windows documentation for configuration details, or call your local Windows dealer for more information.

HELPFUL SUGGESTIONS

If you're using this book as a part of a class, consider the following recommendations:

1. **Follow directions.** The class directions are dictated to you by the instructor. Try to keep up with the class and refrain from experimenting with the software until free time is allowed. This will help the class move through the topics with greatest efficiency.
2. **Study and practice.** Go over the classroom exercises and the supplementary practice exercises at home.
3. **Don't sweat the small stuff.** Depending on the length of the class and the average learning curve, you may not get through all the material. Just be sure to take the time to finish the Web Site Development Form as soon as you can. This provides you with the framework to continue developing your Web presentation.

ACKNOWLEDGMENTS

A book of this nature is the result of collaborative effort. Sincere appreciation is extended to the many brave students who inspired the development of this book. Also thanks to the Franklin, Beedle and Associates, Inc., team: Samantha Soma, Bill DeRouchey, Tom Sumner, and Steve Klinetobe, as well as Jim, Dan, Vic, Karen, Sue, Laura, Eric, Ann, and Chris who advised, pushed, corrected, and generally displayed great patience with me. Thanks also to Elizabeth von Radics for her careful manuscript editing.

I also want to mention my dog, Herman, who unselfishly posed for the tutorial graphic files with no thought of fame and fortune. (Well, maybe not fortune.) Most important, my husband, Dan Barrett, should be acknowledged for his steadfast support of an overtaxed, often grumpy writer whose idea of a really good time is eating salsa and watching bad horror movies.

Dawn Groves
email: dawng@skycat.com
home page: http://www.skycat.com/~dawng/dawn.html

CONTENTS

THE WEB PAGE WORKBOOK

INTRODUCTION

This book is designed for the beginning Web page designer. It provides all the information necessary to design effective, good-looking Web pages in a minimum amount of time. The book can be used with any Web browser and comes bundled with EarthLink's TotalAccess package. It also includes HotDog, a superior shareware Hypertext Markup Language (HTML) editor. You're encouraged to develop your Web pages locally (offline) and then upload them to a Web server when you're ready.

The book is divided into two major sections. The first section describes the Internet, the Web, and Web pages in general. It also contains a simple, practical HTML tutorial that you should be able to complete in a few hours. The second section describes how to design a Web presentation and what kind of information is best presented on the Web. It also offers a variety of helpful tips to make your Web page stand out. A Web site prototype development form is included.

The appendices of this book are filled with useful reference material. Appendix A is a detailed table of HTML 2.0 (and many proposed HTML 3.0 and Netscape-specific) tags. Appendix B summarizes how (and where) to advertise your Web page and how to continue improving your HTML skills; it also suggests additional reference sources. Appendix C is a table of HTML special characters and entities. Appendix D explains how to install the software that accompanies this book. Appendix E describes the use of tables and backgrounds.

WHAT IS THE INTERNET?

The Internet is a worldwide, noncommercial, freely accessible network of computer networks. It's the mother of all computer networks.

The Internet was a 1969 Department of Defense (DoD) military baby, weighing in at four computers. Originally conceived as ARPANET (Advanced Research Projects Administration Network), it was developed to experiment with networks and to share resources among DoD-funded research contractors. As ARPANET matured, universities everywhere were clamoring to sign up. It eventually evolved into two formidable military and nonmilitary computer networks with thousands of smaller networks joining in.

ARPANET aged rapidly under the weight of new technology and the volume of traffic it was managing. The National Science Foundation (NSF) finally came to the rescue, assigning five supercomputers to handle the ever-increasing load. In 1990 when ARPANET ended its reign, NSFNET took over.

Today, NSFNET is phasing itself out, with a variety of commercial and noncommercial networks taking up the cyberspace slack. New networks sponsored by local phone companies and regional providers are springing up around the globe, constantly expanding the scope of Internet traffic. In a short quarter of a century, the Internet has grown from a four-computer twinkle in the DoD's eye into an all-encompassing worldwide presence of incalculable importance.

WHAT IS THE WEB?

The World Wide Web (WWW) is a vast, ever-expanding collection of online documents and information formatted in Hypertext Markup Language (HTML) distributed over the Internet. The Web includes shopping malls filled with virtual retail outlets, private and public repositories of software, libraries, magazines, newspapers, online cafes and meeting spots, forums, and much more. As technology goes, the Web is a relatively young extension of the Internet, created in 1989 at the European Particle Physics Laboratory (CERN) in Geneva, Switzerland. Research scientist Tim Berners-Lee developed the Web to facilitate the sharing of scientific documents and data. Little did he realize that by helping out his physicist pals, he gave birth to one of the fastest-growing data distribution networks the world has ever seen.

The Web is exploding in popularity because of its simple, graphical nature and easy accessibility. Before 1989 only a relatively small community of individuals had the skill to understand and use the Internet. But when the Web was born, suddenly anyone could do it. Instead of cryptic commands, the Web employed simple point-and-click techniques already used in standard online help screens. That is, you could click a visible link and "jump" to the referenced document regardless of its location. No experience necessary.

SO WHAT?

The Internet is an ever-growing electronic universe of at least 15 million subscribers; some statisticians estimate this number at 30 million. The World Wide Web is largely responsible for the most recent explosion of interest and growth. The Web offers unparalleled professional, recreational, and personal development opportunities for both individuals and businesses:

- Tiny startup companies can set up shop on the Web and play with the big boys. With a good Web site, no one knows whether you operate out of a crystal highrise or a suburban garage.

- On the Web you can access many of the best information repositories in the world. The Library of Congress has a Web site, as do most government and educational institutions. Special-interest groups, hobby groups, and non-profit organizations have set up informative Web pages on just about any topic you can imagine. Web research, especially with the development of more-sophisticated retrieval utilities, can be as fruitful as it is convenient.

- Many businesses maintain Web sites. You can quickly find out about new products, download information, learn more about a company, and conduct financial transactions. You can even order pizza.

- If you have something to publish, you can publish it on the Web. We're talking immediate gratification here. Online books and special-interest magazines (known as 'zines) proliferate on the Web. Some of them are even good.

- Many major newspapers and magazines have a Web presence. There are also a variety of excellent news and media sources that are strictly virtual; that is, no physical counterpart whatsoever. You can rise and shine, get your coffee, and read the morning computer.

- A vast number of Web sites encourage you to post your opinions, make suggestions, and ask questions. If you have something to say, there are a thousand places to say it on the Web. If you're still not satisfied, create your own Web page and say it there too.

HOW THE WEB WORKS

The Web is a compendium of virtually countless Web-formatted (HTML) documents, known as Web *pages* (the terms *document* and *page* are often interchangeable). Web documents live on computers that run *HTTP (Hypertext Transfer Protocol) servers.* Most HTTP (Web) servers are hosted on UNIX machines; however, personal computers (PCs) and Macintosh computers are also used. To access a Web server and display a Web page, you need *client* software known as a Web *browser.* Browsers are so named because they are easy-to-use programs that allow you to freely browse Web pages for hours at a time.

Web *links* (also known as *hypertext,* hyperlinks, hotspots, and jumps) are visually distinctive words, phrases, and graphics located on Web pages. In most browsers, links are colored (often blue) and/or underlined. When you select a link on a Web page, the file referenced in the link is downloaded from the server to your computer. Web pages can have any number of links embedded in them, creating an endless web of documents to sample.

Important: This is a deliberately simple explanation of the relationship between HTTP servers and the Web files they access. Servers also run special Common Gateway Interface (CGI) *scripts* which facilitate hypertext connections to local resources such as databases. CGI scripts are discussed later in the book when you learn about imagemaps and forms.

WEB PAGES IN A NUTSHELL

A Web page is simply a document written in the Web-formatting language, HTML. (More on HTML later.) It can be one to many screens in length. When the Web was younger, Web pages offered software download sites and provided Web authors with a cyber soapbox. Now that the commercial nature of the Web is being exploited, Web pages are also used to advertise products, companies, and services. Most corporations are scrambling to create a strong Web presence in an effort to lure even a small percentage of the Web citizenry to their goods.

HOME PAGES

Some Web documents are described using the generic term *home page.* The most commonly referenced home page is the opening document to particular Web site, signifying the top of the site hierarchy and providing a generalized table of contents in the form of links. This could be a business site, such as that for Franklin Beedle &

Associates (`http://www.fbeedle.com`) or a personal site such as my home page (`http://www.skycat.com/~dawng/dawn.html`).

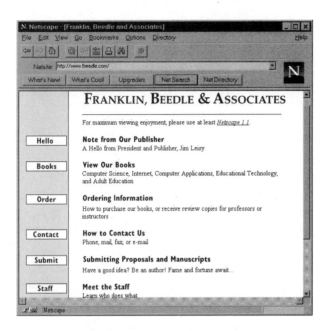

As more people establish a presence on the Web, personal sites are becoming more popular. They can include anything: scanned photos of the family, business information, your spiritual philosophy, a list of prime Web sites, your e-mail address, or your recipe for lasagna.

Most browsers allow to you select a default home page (see page 13), marking a consistent starting place for all of your Web-browsing adventures. Popular default home pages are documents containing a buffet of topics that link all over the Web. The Netscape home page (`http://home.netscape.com`) or the NCSA What's New on the Web page (`http://www.ncsa.uiuc.edu/SDG/Software/Mosaic/Docs/whats-new.html`) frequently serve this function.

FIGURE 2   NETSCAPE HOME PAGE

The home page for this tutorial is a local file (that is, you don't have to go online to retrieve it) called Hello World. As you progress through the book, you'll learn how to load the Hello World home page if it isn't already set as your default home page. Once you have online access established and you've completed the tutorial, you should reset the browser default home page to another Web document such as the Netscape home page, the NCSA What's New home page, or some other interesting spot.

ELEMENTS OF A WEB PAGE

Most Web pages contain three main components formatted in HTML: text, graphics, and links. When you view a Web page in a browser, you see all three elements (the links are usually underlined and in a different color).

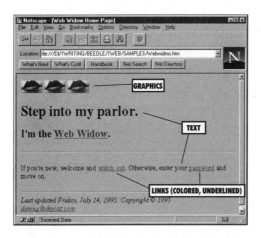

FIGURE 3   THE ELEMENTS OF A WEB PAGE—THE VIEW FROM THE BROWSER

The HTML itself is visible only in an HTML editor or when you look at the page as an ASCII source file.

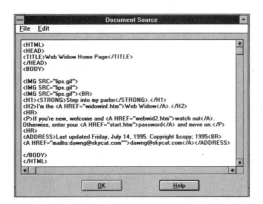

FIGURE 4   THE ELEMENTS OF A WEB PAGE—THE VIEW FROM THE ASCII SOURCE FILE

TEXT

The text is simple 7-bit ASCII, which is best represented by the keys available on a standard keyboard. It's important to note that the extended 8-bit ASCII character set isn't supported by many browsers. The extended set includes special characters such as umlauts and trademark symbols, and varies from font to font, and computer to computer. HTML does provide special codes known as *character entities* that theoretically offer you 8-bit ASCII characters; however, they don't always display correctly on some browsers. More about character entities later in the book. See Appendix C for a complete list of character entity codes.

GRAPHICS

Because the Web invites the use of graphics, most Web pages contain one or more graphic files. There are two ways that the Web traditionally displays graphics: external and inline. An external graphic is associated with a link; it displays only when you click the link. Inline graphics are automatically downloaded as part of the Web page. Graphics are discussed in detail later in the book.

LINKS AND URLS

Links are the transporters of the Web. They seem to effortlessly transport you from one Web document to another regardless of the physical distance. In actuality, links contain addresses of the Web files they're referencing. When you click the link, the address is accessed and the referenced file is downloaded from the server to your screen.

Figure 5 shows a sample page of links.

> ### MULTIPLE MULTIMEDIA
>
> Even though graphics are the most common Web page multimedia insert, they certainly aren't the only type you'll see. More and more, sound and video files are being added to Web documents. The problem is that you must use a program to interpret the sound or run the video. And you may need extra hardware such as a sound card to effectively see or hear the file. But have no fear; you can download shareware multimedia interpreters from a variety of sites. Refer to Appendix B for details. As far as purchasing the extra hardware, well, you're on your own.

In the HTML world, a Web address is known as a *Uniform Resource Locator,* or *URL.* The Cool Site of the Day address, `http://www.infi.net/cool.html`, is a fairly typical-looking Web URL. As ugly as it may be, a URL is easy to interpret once you understand how it's constructed. Think of a URL as organized into three sections—how, where, and what:

```
how you get it://where it is/what you want
```

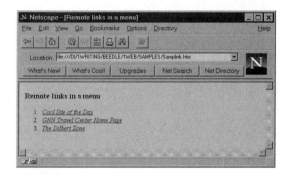

FIGURE 5   SAMPLE LINKS

The link text, Cool Site of the Day, contains the address `http://www.infi.net/cool.html`. You don't necessarily see this address on the displayed Web page, but when you click the link, the `cool.html` file, is downloaded.

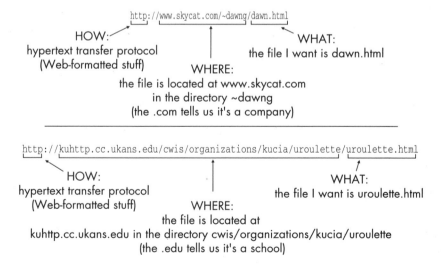

FIGURE 6   THE ORGANIZATION OF A URL

1. **How you get it:**

   This is the method of access. On the Web, the common method of access is HTTP, which stands for Hypertext Transfer Protocol. HTTP is the protocol that moves probably 90 percent of the Web traffic. When you specify HTTP in a URL, you're accessing an HTTP (Web) server.

   Even though most Web traffic travels via HTTP, URLs can contain other server protocols. This allows you to access other forms of data distribution available on the Internet—via the Web. Here's a simplified list of server protocols:

`ftp://`	Access File Transfer Protocol servers (`ftp://domain.edu/path/document.txt`). Browse through directories and transfer files to and from your computer.
`file://`	Access local or networked files, not over the Internet (`file://localserver/directory/file.html`).
`gopher://`	Cruise gopherspace (`gopher://utirc.utoronto.ca/string`). Browse through gopher menus and download files of interest.
`mailto:`	Send electronic mail to the designated mail address (`mailto:dawng@skycat.com`).
`news:`	Access USENET newsgroups (`news:news.group`).
`wais://`	Access Wide Area Network Search (WAIS) databases (`wais://wais.server.edu/database`). Primarily a research utility.
`telnet://`	Log into a host computer (`telnet://server.big.edu`). Your computer functions as a remote terminal.

BE ACCURATE WITH URLS

Make sure you copy a URL exactly as it is referenced. URLs are case-sensitive and inflexible. **http://www.fba.com/fba.html** is not the same as **http://www.fba.com/FBA.html**.

2. **Where it is:**

   This is the location of the Web document you want to see. The location is everything between the colon/slash/slash (`://`) and the last single slash (`/`) in the URL, if a single slash exists. The location usually starts with the name of the HTTP server (the *domain*) and then lists the directory path. The domain name is separated from the directory path by a single slash. Domain names often end with one of the following extensions:

`.com` (a commercial organization)
`.edu` (an educational institution, often a university)
`.org` (a nonprofit organization)
`.gov` (a governmental agency)
`.net` (a networking organization)

The above extensions are occasionally followed by a number (such as `:80`), indicating the server port. If the domain name isn't present, the server defaults to the current Web page's domain. In Figure 6, the domain in the first URL is `www.skycat.com`. The domain in the second URL is `kuhttp.cc.ukans.edu`.

Directory paths can be simple to complex. If a directory path isn't specified after the domain name, the server defaults to its root Web directory. In Figure 6, the directory path in the first URL is `/~dawng/`. The directory path in the second URL is `/cwis/organizations/kucia/uroulette/`. For more details on directory paths, see "Relative versus Absolute Addresses" on pages 66–69.

3. **What you want:**

    In general, this is the filename for the Web document you want to download. The filename is typically the last item in the URL. Web documents usually include an `.htm` extension if they're on PCs and an `.html` (or similar) extension if they're on UNIX machines. If a filename isn't specified in the URL, the server defaults to a document known as an index page in the root Web directory. The index page is like the home page for the Web site.

    Important: The URL doesn't always download a Web document per se. Sometimes the "what you want" portion of the URL points to a Common Gateway Interface (CGI) script. A CGI script is a program (often written in Perl or C) that can perform any number of functions including accessing a database, formatting data into a Web document, and then downloading the results to the browser. CGI scripts are a more advanced implementation of HTML; they're discussed in the "Advanced Topics" section of the book.

Because it's easier to demonstrate the Web than to talk about it, let's move to the next section and get into the browser. Instructions and screen captures in the book reference Netscape Navigator 1.22 for Windows 95; however, any browser will serve well for most of the functions. As you get into newer HTML display options such as backgrounds and tables, you'll want to use a high-end browser that can interpret them.

Important: At this point if you haven't already done so, you should install a Web browser and an HTML editor. The book references Netscape Navigator and includes it with the HTML editor, HotDog, on disk. Refer to Appendix D for installation instruction notes.

WHAT IS A BROWSER?

A Web browser allows you to easily display Web pages and navigate the Web. There are many flavors of Web browsers, but they can be grouped into two basic categories: text-only and graphical.

- Text-only browsers: A text-only browser such as Lynx allows you to view Web pages without showing art or page structure. Essentially, you look at ASCII text on a screen. The advantage of a text-only browser is that it displays Web pages very fast. There's no waiting for multimedia downloads.

- Graphical browsers: To enjoy the multimedia aspect of the Web, you must use a graphical browser such as Netscape Navigator or NCSA Mosaic. Graphical browsers can show pictures, play sounds, and even run video clips. The downside is that multimedia files, particularly graphics, often take a long time to download. Graphical browsers tend to be significantly slower than their text-only counterparts. And this waiting time can be stretched even further with slow connections or heavy online traffic.

MEET THE BROWSER

This section is written with Netscape Navigator 1.22 as the browser of choice. Netscape Navigator is a high-end browser, currently available for downloading from the `http://home.netscape.com` Web site. If you're using another browser, feel free to skip this section. Better yet, take the time to tour your browser's menu items and options even if it isn't Netscape Navigator. Most browsers have similar sorts of functions. *Pay particular attention to the **File, Open File** (sometimes called **Open Local**) and **Reload** commands (or something similar to them); you'll be using them frequently.* Throughout the book I'll be referencing browser functions in very general terms, so regardless of the software you use you should be able to navigate the instructions with little difficulty.

THE INDEX CASE: THE FIRST BROWSER

The first graphical browser, Mosaic, was developed in Illinois at the National Center for Supercomputing Applications (NCSA). It was originally distributed as freeware and, at the time of this writing, continues to be available on the Web at the NCSA home page (**http://www.ncsa.uiuc.edu**). NCSA Mosaic spawned a variety of commercially available clones including Netscape Navigator, Microsoft's Internet Explorer, and many others. Each browser displays Web-formatted documents a little differently. As with all commercial software, every program has its own special features.

PREVENTING THE BROWSER FROM DIALING OUT

For the purposes of this tutorial, you don't need to dial out to the Internet. You'll be developing your Web pages locally (offline) and then viewing them locally using the browser. To prevent the browser from dialing out, either disable the default home page feature or change the default home page from an external file to a local file. Here's how to do it with Netscape 1.22. If you're not using Netscape, chances are your browser will have similar configuration options.

- **Disable the automatic home page load feature:** Select the **Options** menu, **Preferences** command. In the Preferences dialog box, select the **Styles** tab. Under **Window Styles**, choose the **Blank Page** option button. (In Netscape 2.0, the **Blank Page** option button is under **Startup** on the Appearance tab.) This will cause Netscape to start without loading a Web page. The program won't automatically dial out until you enter another URL in the **Location** text box or click the **Home** button on the button bar.

- **Change the default home page:** Select the **Options** menu **Preferences** command. In the Preferences dialog box, select the **Styles** tab. Under **Window Styles**, choose the **Home Page Location** button. (In Netscape 2.0, the **Home Page Location** button is under **Startup** on the Appearance tab.) Type the complete local home page path into the text box (such as `file:///a:⎮hello.htm`). This will cause Netscape to start with a local home page loaded. Netscape won't dial out until you enter a remote URL in the **Location** text box. When you've completed the tutorial and you're ready to automatically link to an online home page, change the **Home Page Location** path to the URL of your online page.

    Important: Note that the home page path is formatted for UNIX. A third backslash (`/`) after `file://` indicates that the subsequent text is a directory path. The bar character (`⎮`) after the drive identifier replaces the standard colon (`:`). (A colon has other meanings in UNIX.)

TOURING NETSCAPE NAVIGATOR'S MENU BAR

You should already have a browser installed and ready to go. If not, refer to Appendix D for installation notes on Netscape Navigator and the HTML editor included with this book, HotDog. This book isn't intended to be a tutorial for Netscape Navigator. Netscape support is available in an online handbook from the Netscape Web site after you install the program.

Now let's take a quick look at Netscape Navigator. Most of the basic Netscape features are available in other browsers. (Certain basic functions are necessary in all browsers.) If you're using a browser other than Netscape, try to locate the commands referenced in the tour below on your particular browser's menu bar.

This book uses Netscape Navigator 1.22 running in Windows 95. If you're running a different version of Netscape, you will notice a few differences in the command sequences. Regardless of which browser you use in what operating environment, it never hurts to keep the software upgraded. Advanced features such as wraparound text, background colors, and tables are constantly being added to browsers. To download the latest Netscape, go to **http://home.netscape.com**.

Ready to get your hands dirty?

Warning: Do not click any of the menu options or buttons without explicit directions to do so. This is because some options may automatically dial out. If you're in a classroom situation, your instructor will tell you what is appropriate. Otherwise, simply follow the instructions as listed below.

1. If the browser isn't already launched, double-click the browser program icon .

2. If your browser is not online, your screen may be blank or you might see the Hello World home page designed for this tutorial (Figure 7).

3. If the opening screen is anything other than the Welcome home page, open the local HTML file a:\hello.htm. To do this in Netscape, select the **File** menu **Open File** command. In the Open File dialog box, open a:\hello.htm.

4. Your browser should be displaying the Welcome home page. If it isn't, go back to step 3.

5. Let's tour the browser menus. First, click the **File** menu.

The **File** menu allows you to create a new window, open a different Web location URL (address), open a local Web page file on your computer (we'll be doing this throughout the tutorial), save the content area of the current Netscape page in HTML format or plain text, send mail, read about the properties of the current Web page, view lists of favorite URLs (hotlists), and print Web pages. You can also close individual windows from this menu or exit the browser entirely. And, perhaps most important, you can view the original HTML version (the document source code) of any Web page you see. (In Netscape 2.0, the **Document Source** command is in the **View** menu.)

FIGURE 7   NETSCAPE WINDOW

6. Click the **Edit** menu.

The **Edit** menu lets you cut, copy, and paste selected text to the Windows Clipboard and find any specified text string in a displayed Web page. You can also undo the last action you performed.

7. Click the **View** menu.

The **View** menu lets you reload a fresh copy of the current page to replace the original. It also enables automatic viewing of images on the current Web page in case the **Options** menu **Auto Load Images** command is disabled. The **Source** command produces a dialog box displaying the HTML source of the current Web page.

8. Click the **Go** menu.

The **Go** menu helps you move backward and forward through Web pages, jumps to your default home page, stops the current Web page from loading, and views a history of your current session Web travel. (In Netscape 2.0, the **History** command is in the **Windows** menu.)

9. Click the **Bookmarks** menu.

Bookmarks keep track of Web page titles that you would like to visit again. In other browsers, these are called hotlists. Netscape Navigator lets you easily add bookmarks and create "folders" to organize them. If you're in a classroom and there are bookmarks listed, *do not click* them. The class is designed to run offline, and if the bookmark references an online URL, Netscape Navigator will automatically try to dial out.

10. Click the **Options** menu.

The **Options** menu lets you customize aspects of Netscape Navigator's operations. You can set preferences for window styles, link styles, fonts, colors, mail, news, cache, network, applications, directories, images, security, proxies, and helper applications. You can also toggle the visibility of the toolbar, Location text box, directory buttons, and the automatic display of images as a Web page is downloaded to your screen. The **Save Options** command lets you save the selected options as defaults for subsequent Netscape sessions.

11. Click the **Directory** menu.

The **Directory** menu is a hotlist of links specific to Netscape. If you're not online or if you're in a classroom situation, *do not click* any of these selections, because they will automatically dial out.

12. Click the **Help** menu.

The **Help** menu provides online help for the various functions available in Netscape Navigator. Specifically, the Handbook is the user manual for the browser. If you're not online or if you're in a classroom situation, *do not click* these selections unless instructed to do so. Some options automatically dial out.

THE TOOLBAR

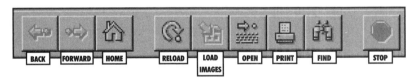

| BACK | FORWARD | HOME | RELOAD | LOAD IMAGES | OPEN | PRINT | FIND | STOP |

FIGURE 8   NETSCAPE NAVIGATOR TOOLBAR

The toolbar automates many of the commonly used functions available in the menus. When you rest your mouse pointer on a toolbar button, you'll see a "tooltip" identifying that button.

- The **Back** button moves you to the previously displayed Web page. If the **Back** button is dimmed, there is no previously displayed Web page to load.

- The **Forward** button moves you to the next Web page in the list of pages you've already seen. If the **Forward** button is dimmed, you're at the end of the list.

- The **Home** button loads the default home page (see page 13). If the default home page isn't local, Netscape Navigator will automatically dial out.

- The **Reload** button reloads the current Web page. This is the button you'll use to update Web pages once they've been edited and saved in the HTML editor.

- The **Load Images** button displays inline images as they download into your browser.

- The **Open** button displays a dialog box that lets you enter a Web page URL.

- The **Print** button sends the current Web page to the printer.

- The **Find** button lets you search for text strings in the current Web page.

- The **Stop** button cancels the current task. This is useful when you're downloading a Web document and you want to cancel the download.

THE DIRECTORY BUTTONS

| What's New! | What's Cool! | Upgrades | Net Search | Net Directory | Newsgroups |

FIGURE 9   NETSCAPE NAVIGATOR DIRECTORY BAR

Directory buttons display online pages of information that help you browse the Internet. Many of these pages are located at the Netscape Web site.

- The **What's New!** button lists the newest, most interesting Web sites.

- The **What's Cool!** button lists the coolest Web sites, not all of them new.

- The **Upgrades** button connects you to a page where you can upgrade Netscape.

- The **Net Search** button lets you conduct online searches for information.

- The **Net Directory** button connects you to various directories for exploring the Internet.

- The **Newsgroups** button helps you explore USENET newsgroups.

- The **Handbook** button displays Netscape's online browser support documentation.

TOURING A LOCAL WEB SITE

With Hello World onscreen, you'll notice a link to The Blues Café (`a:\blues\index.htm`). This is a small sample Web site that you can use to practice some of Netscape's commands. When you create your own Web site, you'll be able to navigate through it in a similar manner. The advantage to keeping your site local is that you can edit, add to, and debug it easily, until you're ready to up-load it for the world to enjoy. Remember, use any of the navigation buttons and commands, but don't click on bookmarked sites that will cause you to dial out.

INTRODUCING HTML

You're impatient. You're ready to start building a Web page *now*. But before you begin any kind of construction, you must know what tools and materials to use. In the case of Web pages, your tools include the Hypertext Markup Language (HTML), an HTML editor program or word processor, and a browser. Your building material is simple ASCII text.

WHAT IS HTML?

HTML is the source language of every Web-formatted document. A Web-format-ted document is an ASCII text file punctuated with HTML *tags*. Tags are HTML labels enclosed in angle brackets, such as `<HR>` and `<HTML>`. Tags identify *structural elements* such as links, headings, subheadings, body text paragraphs, numbered and indented lists, line breaks, and so on. Tags also indicate where to insert graphics, how to emphasize characters, where to include fill-in forms, and where to insert horizontal lines. Most tags come in pairs, also known as *containers* because they mark the beginning and ending of elements. For example, the text contained in the tag pair `<H1>...</H1>` is a level 1 heading element. Some tags are single, such as `<HR>`, which stands for the horizontal rule element.

Elements tagged in HTML can be interpreted and displayed by any Web browser on any Web-compliant platform. For example, when an element is tagged as a level 1 heading, the browser checks its internal description of a level 1 heading (such as 18-point, bold, Times New Roman) and then displays the element accordingly. Even though a level 1 heading may look different in various browsers, it will usually demonstrate its hierarchical position by being bigger than the associated subhead-ings and body text. Note that in Figures 10 and 11, the same elements display differ-ently in the two different browser windows.

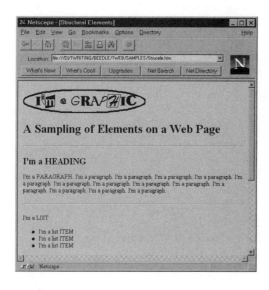

THE HTML PHILOSOPHY

In a nutshell, HTML philosophy professes that structure is more important than layout. In other words, you should compose HTML documents based on how you want the information structured and *not* by how you want it to visually appear onscreen. So even though HTML lets you "tag" document text, indicating what element (paragraph, numbered list, heading) it should be, the tags don't generally include layout information. This is difficult to understand because most of us think about how something looks, not how it's built. But because HTML is platform-independent, each browser interprets the layout of the tagged elements differently. The browser has control over how the document looks. You have control only over how the document is structured.

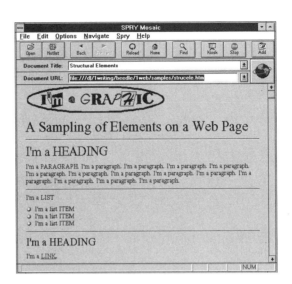

FIGURE 11   STRUCTURAL ELEMENTS IN SPRY MOSAIC

In HTML philosophy, you shouldn't plan on how a Web document is going to display, because there are so many ways it can be interpreted. You can't guarantee that a level 1 heading will always be a certain size and font choice. What you *can* guarantee is that each platform will display the structural elements in a locally consistent, logical manner. You know that a level 1 heading will always be a dominant element, clearly emphasized over lower-level headings and body text. The integrity of your document's structure will always be maintained, even if the font sizes and styles differ from computer to computer and browser to browser.

HTML philosophy also advises you to avoid the fancy HTML tag extensions that require specific browsers. You should use only standardized HTML based on the latest version. (Right now that's HTML 2.0; some HTML 3.0 is in use but it hasn't yet been standardized.) Always remember that when you use customized tags or fancy extensions, you effectively exclude everyone who doesn't use the specific browser you're writing to. You're no longer platform-independent. Your Web page may look crummy on a lot of browsers.

DIFFERENT TYPES OF HTML EDITORS

You don't need any special kind of software to generate HTML documents, beyond a simple text editor that will save your ASCII text file. That being said, an *HTML editor* is helpful because it simplifies the task by not requiring you to remember tag names. For example, instead of typing the tag pair `<A HREF=" "></A>`, you can click a button or select a command. Currently, most HTML editors are shareware programs, such as the editor included with this book, HotDog. For a list of other shareware editors, visit HTML online resource sites referenced in Appendix B.

By the time this book is published, most high-end word processors will probably include HTML add-on programs such as the Word for Windows HTML Assistant. These add-ons allow you to format the HTML elements visually, the same way you'd format any document. You don't work directly with tags. It's pretty close to WYSIWYG editing, because you see the elements looking very much like they'll look when the document is published on the Web. Sounds easy, right?

Currently, the problem with these add-ons is that they access a subset of HTML. Because you can't work directly with tags, you can't harness all the features HTML offers. Bottom line: If you're going to author Web pages, you really need to understand HTML tags themselves. HTML tags aren't difficult to use; you shouldn't want to be protected from seeing or using them.

> **STRUCTURE AND LAYOUT**
>
> The distinction between structure and layout can be difficult to grasp because most of us tend to think in terms of appearance.
>
> - *Structure* describes the elements that make up the document. These elements include paragraphs, six levels of headings, three types of lists, citations, addresses, four kinds of links, and much more. Structure doesn't concern itself with the appearance of the elements. It only dictates their organizational hierarchy relative to each other (level 1 headings are higher up the ladder than level 2 and 3 headings, for example).
>
> - *Layout* describes elements in terms of appearance. With layout, you not only identify a paragraph as an element of a document, you also specify the element's appearance—indentation values, font, and point size.

ALL ABOUT TAGS

Just as styles are the workhorses of word processors, tags are the workhorses of HTML. They identify the structural elements of a document, such as levels of headings, paragraphs, various types of lists, links to other documents or images, forms and imagemaps, and a few (very few) visual format preferences. Tags that aren't understood by browsers are ignored.

Here are some important facts about HTML tags:

- Tags are enclosed in left and right angle-brackets: `<tag>`. This is how browsers distinguish between the ASCII text `"HTML"` and the tag `<HTML>`.

BROWSER-SPECIFIC DESIGN

On the Web you'll frequently run across sites that are designed for specific browsers. There's a lot of controversy in the HTML authoring community about this. Some browsers can interpret newer, more dynamic tags, making their Web pages more visually stimulating. The problem, once again, goes back to philosophy. When you design for appearance (which many of these gee-whiz tags are created for), you distance yourself from the platform-independent, structure-oriented foundation of HTML.

Try not to become entranced with browser-specific enhancements. Human nature being what it is, people tend to bore easily of these bells and whistles. You're better off spending time on *content*. The pages that wear the longest are multi-browser compatible, contemporary looking, easy to use, and contain good solid content. See "Confessions of an HTML Heretic" in Appendix B.

- Tags are case-insensitive. It doesn't matter whether you type <HTML>, <html>, or <HtmL>. However, for ease of use and consistency, choose a case preference and stick with it. Tags are capitalized in this book.

- Many tags come in pairs. For example, the <H1> *start tag* indicates the beginning of a level 1 heading element, and the </H1> *end tag* indicates the end of the same element. The text sandwiched between the two tags is the actual heading text. (Note the slash symbol [/] identifying the end tag.)

- Some tags are single entities, such as <BR>, indicating a line break, or <HR>, indicating a horizontal line. They don't have an end tag.

- Some tags contain *attributes* which modify the start tag in a special way. For example, the IMG (image) tag <IMG SRC="*image URL*"> includes the mandatory attribute SRC, indicating that the address following the tag is a URL. Some attributes are mandatory; most are optional.

- Tags must be correctly positioned relative to other tags as well as the text they're modifying. For example, a paragraph <P>...</P> element isn't legal unless it's nested inside of <BODY>...</BODY> tags. Appendix A lists the standard HTML tags along with their correct positioning.

As you create your first HTML document, you'll learn about the various types of tags and how they're used. But before you jump in, let's briefly get acquainted with the HTML editor, HotDog. If you haven't already launched your HTML editor, please do so now. If you're not using an HTML editor, launch whatever word processor you're going to use. Keep in mind that unless otherwise indicated, the sample screens you see in the book are of the HotDog HTML editor, and the Netscape Navigator 1.22 browser.

MEET THE HTML EDITOR

If you're using an HTML editor other than Sausage Software's HotDog, feel free to skip this section. Better yet, take a minute to explore the limits of your selected editor. HTML editors span a wide range of capabilities.

HotDog is a high-end editor with good online help and a variety of time-saving tag-insertion features. Even though you'll be typing the tags to facilitate learning them, feel free to use HotDog's menu options, dialog boxes, and quick-format buttons. You'll notice that HotDog includes many HTML 3.0 tags not described in the tutorial. (Many HTML 3.0 tags are listed in Appendix A.) If you're using an editor other than HotDog, you should still be able to navigate the tutorial with little difficulty.

Now, let's take a look at HotDog (refer to Appendix D for installation notes). If you're in a classroom situation, you probably already have HotDog installed and ready to go. Note that this book isn't intended to be a HotDog tutorial. At some point you should take the time to explore HotDog's online tutorial and help documentation.

IT MAY BE LIMITED, BUT IT'S EVOLVING

HTML is a young, evolving language currently in its second release, HTML 2.0. There's a third release in the works. Each release offers new tags and enhancements. Many HTML 3.0 tags, as well as specialized extensions, are already functioning in high-end browsers (such as Netscape Navigator). As browsers are upgraded, more and more of these enhancements will be used. Though much of the tutorial portion of this primer concentrates on basic HTML 2.0, you'll find some HTML 3.0 and Netscape-specific tags included in Appendix A.

IT AIN'T FREE

Netscape and Sausage Software offer free access to their programs for a limited time. If you like the programs and plan to continue using them, please register appropriately.

1. If HotDog isn't already running, choose **Run** from the **File** menu or **Start** button and key in **c:\hotdog\hotdog.exe**.

2. If HotDog queries you about registering, click the **OK** button when it becomes active.

3. If HotDog presents a Welcome dialog box, click the **Use HotDog Now** button.

   HotDog opens with a default untitled file open and basic HTML tags as shown in Figure 12.

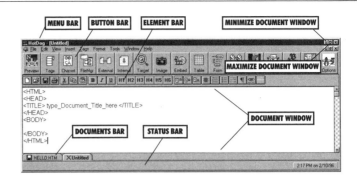

FIGURE 12   HOTDOG OPENING SCREEN

Note: You can change this default option in the **Tools** menu Options dialog box.

4. Let the mouse cursor briefly pause over buttons on the button bar and the element bar below it. Notice the ToolTips identifying the names the buttons.

5. Let's tour the menus. First, click the **File** menu.

The **File** menu contains file management commands such as New, Open, Save, and Close. It also controls printing, lets you preview the current file on a default browser, and has a special Publish (similar to Save) feature that prepares files for uploading to a UNIX server. (Use the Publish feature when your Web pages are complete and ready for transfer.)

6. Click the **Edit** menu.

The **Edit** menu contains editing commands such as Undo, Cut, Copy, Paste, and Append. It also includes Find and Replace features.

7. Click the **View** menu.

The **View** menu lets you toggle on and off the HotDog button, elements, document, and status bars. It contains two tables of tags and character entities for easy insertion into your document and also accesses the HotDog File Manager.

8. Click the **Insert** menu.

The **Insert** menu facilitates quick insertion of a variety of links as well as tables, lists, horizontal lines, and URLs.

9. Click the **Tags** menu.

The **Tags** menu lets you list all of the available tags. By clicking a tag name, you insert it into the document.

10. Click the **Format** menu.

    The **Format** menu lets you specify <HEAD> and <BODY> formats as well as style tags.

11. Click the **Tools** menu.

    The **Tools** menu contains the Options dialog box, which lets you customize how HotDog manages your HTML files. It also lets you remove hypertext links, HTML tags, and duplicate links from selected text.

12. Click the **Window** menu.

    The **Window** menu lets you arrange open windows and document icons.

13. Click the **Help** menu.

    The **Help** menu contains online help for HotDog's many features. It also contains a simple HTML tutorial.

CREATING YOUR FIRST HTML DOCUMENT

It's time to create a sample HTML document. Finally! First we'll practice the basics. Once you've learned about the tags, you'll read more theory about good Web page design. Then you can start designing you own personal page.

BEGIN AT THE BEGINNING

Every HTML document starts with an <HTML> start tag and ends with an </HTML> end tag. These two tags identify the text between them as HTML formatted. Everything you type from here on will be nested inside this tag pair.

You can't add white space to an HTML document by pressing the spacebar, pressing TAB, or adding blank lines. HTML doesn't recognize white space unless it's in a preformatted paragraph. (<PRE> tags are discussed later in the book.)

Inside the <HTML>...</HTML> tag pair is the <HEAD>...</HEAD> pair and then the <BODY>...</BODY> pair. The <HEAD> and <BODY> tag pairs effectively divide the document into two sections: the head and the body.

> **NO ROOM FOR MISTAKES**
>
> HTML is an unforgiving language. Any typographical error will render a tag invisible to the browser. Some HTML editors include built-in error-checking logic that doesn't allow you to save a document containing format mistakes. HotDog has no resident error-checker. However, shareware HTML verification programs are available online. (Weblint is a good one for the PC.) Regardless, type carefully and check for typos. If you don't catch them in HotDog, you'll certainly see them when you view the page in a browser window.

◎ *Head and Title:* The `<HEAD>...</HEAD>` tag pair can include a variety of optional information which we'll go into later. For now, the most important element in the `<HEAD>` tag pair is the `<TITLE>` tag for your page. The title is important because search tools often index pages by their titles. The title should be short and descriptive of the page content. (For example, "Northwest Dogs Home Page" is more descriptive than "Dogs.") Often the title matches the first heading in the body of document. If your page is part of a multipage site, the title should also include a site identifier. (For example, "Northwest Dogs: Grooming Huskies.") Though the title doesn't usually display on the Web page itself, browsers often display it in a separate text box or include it as part of the window title.

◎ *Body:* The `<BODY>...</BODY>` tag pair includes all other elements: headings, paragraphs, lists, graphics, links—you name it.

The structure of these tags never changes. It's the first thing you type when you create a Web page. (In some HTML editors, such as HotDog, these tags are automatically entered when you create a new document.) The format is as follows:

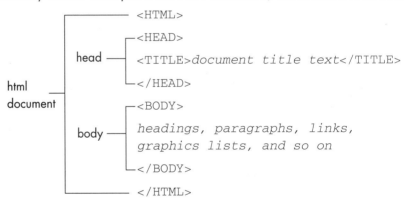

```
                              <HTML>
                           ┌─<HEAD>
                 head ──── │ <TITLE>document title text</TITLE>
                           └─</HEAD>
    html
    document ───
                           ┌─<BODY>
                 body ──── │ headings, paragraphs, links,
                           │ graphics lists, and so on
                           └─</BODY>
                              </HTML>
```

PRACTICE

Let's see how this looks onscreen and add a title.

1. In HotDog, if the following tags aren't already entered, click the **New** button [ ] or choose **File, New**. If you're not using an editor that inserts these tags automatically, type them as follows:

    <HTML>

    <HEAD>

    <TITLE>type document title here</TITLE>

```
</HEAD>

<BODY>

</BODY>

</HTML>
```

Important: HotDog users will notice that default HTML documents contain a `<!DOCTYPE HTML PUBLIC "-//IETF/DTD HTML 3.0//EN" "HTML.dtd">` tag above the `<HTML>` start tag. This is a comment and will not display in the browser. It exists for information purposes only and is not currently required.

2. Type *The Dog Page* inside the `<TITLE>`. . . `</TITLE>` tag pair.

```
<HTML>

<HEAD>

<TITLE>The Dog Page</TITLE>

</HEAD>

<BODY>

</BODY>

</HTML>
```

Note: Because HTML doesn't recognize or care about line breaks and blank lines (unless they're so tagged), the following document is perfectly legal (but harder to edit) as a continuous string of text. The example above can be entered as follows:

```
<HTML><HEAD><TITLE>The Dog Page
</TITLE></HEAD><BODY></BODY></HTML>
```

ADDING HEADINGS AND PARAGRAPHS

Headings and paragraphs are all inside the `<BODY>` of the page. When you specify a heading or a paragraph, you are indicating a structural element. The browser software determines the appearance. If you press Enter to insert blank lines between headings and paragraphs, the browser will ignore them. Use blank lines to enhance the readability of the HTML file itself, but don't expect them to show up in the browser window.

ADDING COMMENTS

Comments can be typed inside a comment tag **<!-- comment text here -->** and inserted anywhere in an HTML document. If your comment is more than one line, place start **<!--** and end **-->** comment brackets around each line. Avoid placing HTML tags inside of comment brackets because the extra angle brackets can confuse some browsers.

Good:

<!-- updated September 5 -->

<!-- need more dog-->
<!-- publication references-->
<!-- found here-->

Bad:

<!-- Ozzie says change tag to <UL> but I disagree -->

<!-- Each comment line must have its own start and end comment tags. -->

ADDING HEADINGS

There are six levels of HTML headings. Each heading is indicated by a tag pair numbered H1 through H6 as follows:

<H1>*level 1 heading text*</H1>

<H2>*level 2 heading text*</H2>

<H3>*level 3 heading text*</H3>

<H4>*level 4 heading text*</H4>

<H5>*level 5 heading text*</H5>

<H6>*level 6 heading text*</H6>

Heading levels are differentiated from each other and the paragraph text by typeface, point size, and extra space above or below the elements. As with all tag pairs, if you don't include the end tag (/), the browser will think that the subsequent text is formatted as part of the heading.

In Netscape Navigator, the six levels of headings look like Figure 13.

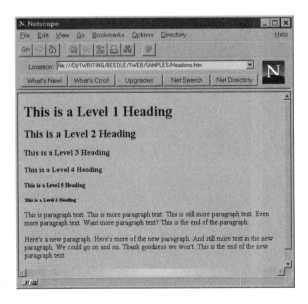

FIGURE 13   HEADINGS IN NETSCAPE NAVIGATOR

Add a level 1 heading to your new document:

3. Type the following level 1 heading into your document.

```
<HTML>

<HEAD>

<TITLE>The Dog Page</TITLE>

</HEAD>

<BODY>

<H1>THE DOG PAGE</H1>

</BODY>

</HTML>
```

ADDING PARAGRAPHS

Paragraph tags are `<P>` and, optionally, `</P>`. As with heading text, paragraph text looks different from browser to browser. Typically, paragraphs are not indented, and a single blank line is inserted between them. The format is as follows:

```
<P>paragraph text
```

or

```
<P>paragraph text</P>
```

`<P>` tags cannot include heading tags, but they can include links and various forms of styles (covered later in the book). Currently, a closing `</P>` tag isn't required in standard HTML, but rumor has it that it may become standard in later versions. Further, some browsers do allow modification of `<P>` tags, necessitating a closing `</P>`. Samples in this book will include `</P>` tags even though they are optional (and sometimes add a little extra white space between paragraphs).

4. Add the following paragraph text to your document.

```
<HTML>

<HEAD>

<TITLE>The Dog Page</TITLE>

</HEAD>
```

```
<BODY>

<H1>THE DOG PAGE</H1>
```

<P>Dogs are fascinating animals. So are cats and iguanas; but this is a dog page, not a cat and iguana page.</P>

```
</BODY>

</HTML>
```

SAVING THE DOCUMENT

In most cases, you must save an HTML document before you view it in the browser. The Save function is standardized in most software. (It's a good idea to save all of your Web site files in a single directory for easy referencing. More information on file organization will be presented later.)

Note: HotDog contains a Preview feature that launches the browser specified in the Options dialog box and displays a temporary version of the current document. The Preview feature doesn't work with all browsers. Instead of using Preview, we'll save the document in HotDog when we're ready to view it, and use the **Reload** button in Netscape Navigator to display the updated file.

PRACTICE

Save the document on drive A.

> 5. Select **Save** (usually located in the **File** menu).
>
> 6. Insert your student diskette into drive A.
>
> 7. Name the file a:\doghome.htm.

VIEWING THE DOCUMENT

As you create your Web page, you should view it frequently in the browser window. This helps you catch mistakes early in the game, before the page gets too complicated. If possible, keep the editor and the browser open so you can switch between them as necessary. (Use the Alt + Tab key combination to easily alternate between the two.)

VIEWING THE FINISHED WEB PAGE

To view the Web page as it'll appear on the Web, launch your browser and open the local HTML document you just created. This is known as opening a local file, because you're not going online to access it.

PRACTICE

Open the file as a local document.

1. If necessary, launch the browser.

2. Open your local HTML document, `a:\doghome.htm`. In Netscape Navigator, click the **File** menu **Open File** command and select the file. Correctly formatted, the page should resemble Figure 14.

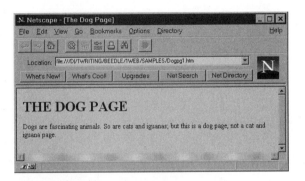

FIGURE 14   THE DOG PAGE, VERSION 1

If the screen doesn't match the figure, return to the editor and check that all your tag pairs are closed properly and typed correctly. Save the document and then view the updated version by selecting the **Reload** button in the browser.

VIEWING THE DOCUMENT SOURCE

The source is simply the HTML text file with all the codes revealed. Remember what you typed in your editor? That's the source. Most browsers let you view the HTML source for any Web document you display. This is useful because you can study how other Web pages are structured.

Browsers usually contain a View Document Source command. In Netscape Navigator, choose the **View** menu **Source** command to display the source of the currently displayed Web page.

FILENAMES: UNIX, PC, OR MAC?

More than likely, your published Web site will be run on a UNIX machine. As such, there are a few simple naming conventions to follow:

@ Stick to the file-naming conventions for your home computer since you'll be testing your files locally. When the documents are published on a UNIX server, their extensions need to be changed appropriately (see Appendix B, "Getting It Up and Out").

@ If you're working on a PC, give your files an **.htm** extension. If you're working on UNIX, give your files an **.html** extension. Other extensions such as **.shtml** exist, but we'll stick with the basics for now.

@ Because UNIX filenames are case-sensitive (**Doghome.htm** and **doghome.htm** are two different files), choose a case preference—upper, lower, or mixed—and stick with it.

Open a document source window to view the `doghome.htm` HTML file.

1. With `doghome.htm` currently displayed in your browser, choose **View**, **Source** to display the source code.

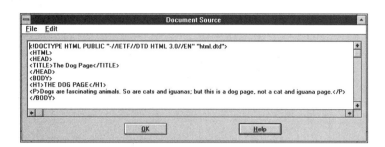

FIGURE 15   THE DOG PAGE, DOCUMENT SOURCE

2. In Netscape Navigator click the **OK** button at the bottom of the document source window to close it and return to the doghome window.

ADDING LEVEL 2 AND 3 HEADINGS

Let's beef up `doghome.htm` by adding a level 2 heading `<H2>...</H2>`, a couple of level 3 headings `<H3>...</H3>`, and more paragraph text. When you view the document in the browser, notice the font differences among the heading levels.

Insert level 2 and level 3 headings into the document as follows:

1. Switch to the HTML editor window (which should still contain doghome.htm) and add the following text:

    ```
    <HTML>

    <HEAD>

    <TITLE>The Dog Page</TITLE>

    </HEAD>

    <BODY>

    <H1>The Dog Page</H1>

    <P>Dogs are fascinating animals. So are cats and
    ```

```
iguanas; but this is a dog page, not a cat and
iguana page.</P>
```

```
<H2>The most popular dog breeds</H2>
```

```
<P>According to Sleeping Dogs, Inc. the most
popular dog breeds are terriers, retrievers,
bulldogs, collies, and poodles.</P>
```

```
<H3>My favorite dog</H3>
```

```
<P>My favorite dog is Herman, a silly looking
mutt with the body of a golden retriever and the
legs of a basset hound.</P>
```

```
<H3>Mom's favorite dog</H3>
```

```
<P>Mom's favorite dog is Sam, a sweet, hairy
little sheltie. Unfortunately, Sam is no longer
with us.</P>
```

```
</BODY>
```

```
</HTML>
```

2. Save `a:\doghome.htm`.
3. Switch to the browser window. In the browser, select **Reload** or **File, Open File** (or an equivalent command) to reload the updated `doghome.htm`. The page should resemble Figure 16.

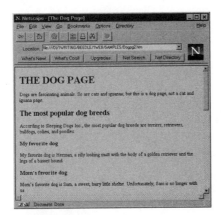

FIGURE 16   THE DOG PAGE, VERSION 2

LISTS AND STYLES

HTML defines three types of lists to help organize Web page information. HTML also provides character styles to emphasize text and horizontal rules to mark sections of the document. Remember, these structures should be used to make documents easier to understand, not just to make them prettier. If you needlessly complicate your page with unnecessary elements, you'll drive Web cruisers away instead of inviting them in.

ADDING LISTS

The more effectively you use lists, the easier it will be for readers to scan your Web page. Fortunately, HTML allows you to structure three different kinds of lists, each with its own identifying tag pair. Early HTML defines two other list structures—see Appendix A; however, the following are the most common:

- ❧ The ordered list (usually numbered) `<OL>...</OL>`
- ❧ The unordered list (usually bulleted) `<UL>...</UL>`
- ❧ The definition list `<DL>...</DL>`

Ordered and unordered list items are individually tagged `<LI>`. Definition list items are alternately tagged as terms `<DT>` and then definitions `<DD>`.

Lists can also be nested in each other as Figure 17 demonstrates.

ADDING AN ORDERED LIST

An ordered list `<OL>...</OL>` is usually numbered. Each item in an ordered list is indicated by the list item tag `<LI>`. Some browsers let you specify the font or style of the numbers. Numbered lists commonly denote an order of presentation or appearance. A simple example would be a recipe or directions to party.

The HTML for the ordered list in Figure 18 is:

```
<H4>Winter bird pudding</H4>

<P>Helps birds survive freezing temperatures.</P>

<OL>

    <LI>Melt 1 cup of butter or margarine into 2 quarts of water.

    <LI>When water boils, add 4 cups (total) any combination of rolled oats, cream of wheat, and cornmeal. Cook until thick, no more than 20 minutes.
```

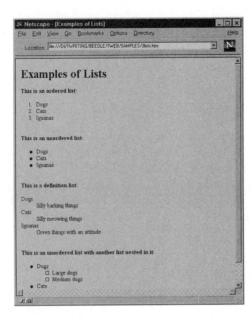

FIGURE 17 THREE LIST EXAMPLE

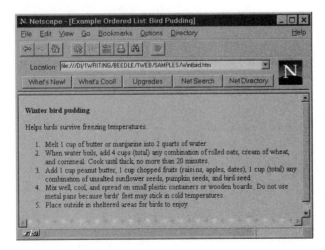

FIGURE 18 ORDERED LIST EXAMPLE

<LI>Add 1 cup peanut butter, 1 cup chopped fruits (raisins, apples, dates), 1 cup (total) any combination of unsalted sunflower seeds, pumpkin seeds, and bird seed.

<LI>Mix well, cool, and spread on small plastic containers or wooden boards. Do not use metal pans because birds' feet may stick in cold temperatures.

<LI>Place outside in sheltered areas for birds to enjoy.

</OL>

Keep in mind that you don't have to keep the <OL> and </OL> tags on separate lines; it's just easier to see the organization of the list.

PRACTICE

Add an ordered list to the doghome.htm document.

1. In the HTML editor, change the paragraph text as follows. (The indenting helps you edit the text; it doesn't affect the browser display.)

```
<P>According to Sleeping Dogs, Inc. these are the
most popular dog breeds:</P>

<OL>

    <LI>Terriers

    <LI>Retrievers

    <LI>Bulldogs

    <LI>Collies

    <LI>Poodles

</OL>
```

2. Save the document. In HotDog, type Ctrl + S to quickly save it.
3. In the browser, select **Reload** or **File, Open File** (or an equivalent command) to view the list. The page should resemble Figure 19.

ADDING AN UNORDERED LIST

An unordered list <UL>...</UL> is generally indicated with bullets or inline graphics. (We'll discuss inline graphics a little later on.) As with ordered lists, each item is preceded by the <LI> tag. Unordered lists commonly indicate a random order without hierarchy, such as a list of names or dates.

FIGURE 19   THE DOG PAGE, ORDERED LIST

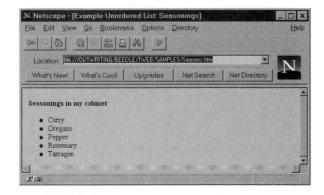

FIGURE 20   UNORDERED LIST EXAMPLE

The HTML for the unordered list shown in Figure 20 is as follows:

```
<H4>Seasonings in my cabinet<H4>

<UL>

    <LI>Curry

    <LI>Oregano

    <LI>Pepper

    <LI>Rosemary

    <LI>Tarragon

</UL>
```

Notice that the ordered and unordered lists have identical HTML with the exception of the `<UL>...</UL>` tag pair for the unordered list.

Let's try this in your `doghome.htm` document.

PRACTICE

Change the ordered list to an unordered list.

1. In the HTML editor, change the ordered list of dog breeds to the following:

```
<P>According to Sleeping Dogs, Inc. these are the
most popular dog breeds:</P>

<UL>

    <LI>Terriers

    <LI>Retrievers

    <LI>Bulldogs

    <LI>Collies

    <LI>Poodles

</UL>
```

2. Save the document. In HotDog, press Ctrl + S to quickly save it.

3. In the browser, select **Reload** or **File**, **Open File** (or an equivalent command) to view the unordered list. (In Netscape, press Ctrl + R to quickly reload.) The page should resemble Figure 21.

FIGURE 21   THE DOG PAGE, UNORDERED LIST

ADDING A NESTED LIST

Lists can be nested inside other lists. To do so, simply create a new list complete with the start and end tags and insert it under the list item you wish to modify. Commonly, list item identifiers (bullets, numbers, and so on) vary as the lists are nested. You can nest any of the three lists inside each other.

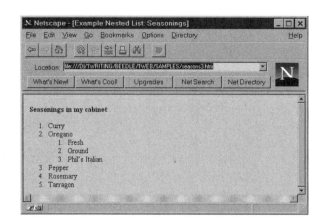

FIGURE 22   **NESTED LIST EXAMPLE**

The nested ordered list in Figure 22 looks like the following in HTML:

```
<H4>Seasonings in my cabinet</H4>

<OL>

    <LI>Curry

    <LI>Oregano

        <OL>

            <LI>Fresh

            <LI>Ground

            <LI>Phil's Italian

        </OL>

    <LI>Pepper

    <LI>Rosemary

    <LI>Tarragon

</OL>
```

Let's try this with unordered lists in your doghome.htm document.

1. In the HTML editor, add a nested unordered list after the first list item, Terriers, as follows:

```
<P>According to Sleeping Dogs, Inc. these are the
most popular dog breeds</P>

<UL>

    <LI>Terriers

        <UL>

            <LI>Small

            <LI>Medium

            <LI>Large

        </UL>

    <LI>Retrievers

    <LI>Bulldogs

    <LI>Collies

    <LI>Poodles

</UL>
```

2. Save the document. In HotDog, press Ctrl+S to quickly save it.

3. In the browser, select **Reload** or **File, Open File** (or an equivalent command) to view the nested list. The page should resemble Figure 23. Notice how the bullet has changed in the nested list. Most browsers vary the bullet characters when an unordered list is nested inside another unordered list.

FIGURE 23   THE DOG PAGE, NESTED UNORDERED LIST

ADDING A DEFINITION LIST

A definition list `<DL>`...`</DL>` has two parts: the term and its definition. The term is preceded by the `<DT>` tag, and its related definition is preceded by the `<DD>` tag. Most browsers display the term on one line and its definition indented on a separate line. Definition lists typically work well for glossaries, but they also serve wherever an indent is needed. The format is as follows:

```
<DL>
     <DT>Term<DD>Definition of term
     <DT>Term<DD>Definition of term
     <DT>Term<DD>Definition of term
</DL>
```

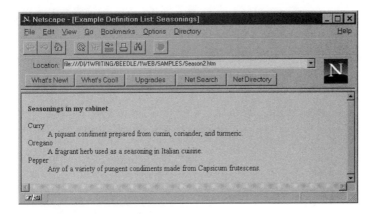

FIGURE 24   DEFINITION LIST EXAMPLE

The HTML for the definition list shown in Figure 24 is as follows:

<H4>Seasonings in my cabinet</H4>

<DL>

    <DT>Curry<DD>A piquant condiment prepared from cumin, coriander, and turmeric.

    <DT>Oregano<DD>A fragrant herb used as a seasoning in Italian cuisine.

    <DT>Pepper<DD>Any of a variety of pungent condiments made from Capsicum frutescens.

</DL>

PRACTICE

Add a defintion list to doghome.htm.

1. In the HTML editor, change the list of dog breeds to the following definition list.

```
<P>According to Sleeping Dogs, Inc. these are the
most popular dog breeds:</P>
```

<DL>

```
<DT>Terriers<DD>A small, active breed of hunt-
ing dog.

<DT>Retrievers<DD>Any of several breeds of dog
that were trained to retrieve game animals.

<DT>Bulldogs<DD>A short-haired dog character-
ized by a large head, strong jaw, and a thick-
set body.

<DT>Collies<DD>A large, agile working dog
originally developed in Scotland as a sheep-
dog.

<DT>Poodles<DD>A non-sporting dog with a dense
coat which can be clipped in a variety of
styles.

</DL>
```

2. Save the document. In HotDog, press Ctrl+S to quickly save it.

3. In the browser, select **Reload** or **File, Open File** (or an equivalent command) to view the definition list. The page should resemble Figure 25.

ADDING A STYLE

HTML style tag pairs add emphasis to characters by assigning them a special meaning or font style. These tags can be nested in most structural elements including paragraphs, headings, lists, and links. Style tags come in pairs, formatting the text between them. The format is `<TAG>text</TAG>`. For example:

```
<P>paragraph text<STRONG>text</STRONG>paragraph
text</P>
```

Nested styles must start and end prior to the end tag of the element they reside in. Correct:

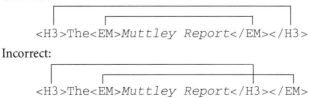

```
<H3>The<EM>Muttley Report</EM></H3>
```

Incorrect:

```
<H3>The<EM>Muttley Report</H3></EM>
```

There are two kinds of style tags: logical and physical.

FIGURE 25   THE DOG PAGE, DEFINITION LIST

LOGICAL STYLE

Logical (soft format) style tags specify how text should be used, but allow the browser to define the appearance of the font. For example, the tag <CITE> is a logical format because it tells the browser to make the text stand out as a citation. Another example is the logical tag <STRONG>; some browsers boldface it and others italicize or underline it. Browsers may render two different logical tags in the same visual format.

Logical tags include <CITE>, <CODE>, <DFN>, <EM>, <KBD>, <SAMP>, <STRIKE>, <STRONG>, and <VAR>. These are demonstrated in Figure 26.

LOGICAL OR PHYSICAL STYLE?

Most HTML tags are logical. They don't specify point size and indentation; they specify structural elements. This ensures a certain local consistency without requiring you to remember font details. Because the majority of HTML tag assignments are already logical, it makes sense to carry this into the application of style tags. Logical styles tags dictate the type of emphasis without specifying the exact way it should look. In keeping with the HTML philosophy, this allows each browser to format the style based on its own capabilities. Consistency is assured. If you assign a physical style tag and the browser can't comply, it'll substitute another font or style with sometimes unattractive or inconsistent results. Generally speaking, it's better to let each browser follow its own rules without trying to micromanage the appearance of the output.

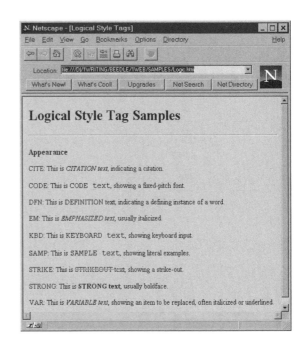

FIGURE 26   LOGICAL STYLE TAGS IN NETSCAPE

PHYSICAL STYLE

Physical (hard format) style tags tell the browser exactly how to display the text. For example, the tag <B> (bold) is a physical format because there's no question as to how the text should appear. Not all browsers can render all physical style tags.

Physical tags include <B>, <I>, and <TT>. These tags are demonstrated in Figure 27.

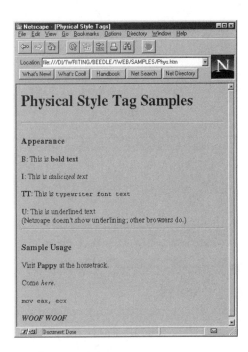

FIGURE 27   PHYSICAL STYLE TAGS IN NETSCAPE

PRACTICE

Add style tags to the dog breed definition list on doghome.htm:

1. In the HTML editor, add the logical style tags <EM> and <STRONG> to the dog breed definition list as follows:

```
<P>According to Sleeping Dogs, Inc. these are
the most <EM>popular</EM>dog breeds:</P>

<DL>

    <DT><STRONG>Terriers</STRONG><DD>A small,
        active breed of hunting dog.
```

```
<DT><STRONG>Retrievers</STRONG><DD>Any of
     several breeds of dog that were trained
     to retrieve game animals.

<DT><STRONG>Bulldogs</STRONG><DD>A short-
     haired dog characterized by a large
     head, strong jaw, and a thickset body.

<DT><STRONG>Collies</STRONG><DD>A large,
     agile working dog originally developed
     in Scotland as a sheepdog.

<DT><STRONG>Poodles</STRONG><DD>A non-
     sporting dog with a dense coat which
     can be clipped in a variety of styles.

</DL>
```

2. Save the document. In HotDog, press Ctrl + S to quickly save it.
3. In the browser, select **Reload** or **File**, **Open File** (or an equivalent command) to view the definition list. The page should resemble Figure 28.

ADDING HORIZONTAL RULES

A horizontal rule is a thin line that runs horizontally across the width of the browser window. Horizontal rules effectively divide a Web page into subsections, making it easier to navigate. A rule is inserted by the addition of a single tag, <HR>. Some browsers permit this tag to be modified for size and width of the line (see Appendix A). This is not, however, standardized HTML 2.0.

PRACTICE

Add two horizontal rules to help The Dog Page seem more orderly:

1. In the HTML editor, insert <HR> tags after the <H1> heading, before the <H2> heading, and before the first <H3> heading.

```
<HTML>

<HEAD>

<TITLE>The Dog Page</TITLE>

</HEAD>

<BODY>

<H1>THE DOG PAGE</H1>
```

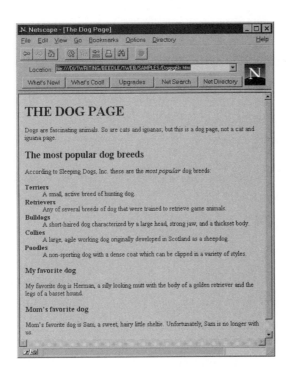

FIGURE 28   THE DOG PAGE, LOGICAL STYLE TAGS

```
<HR>

<P>Dogs are fascinating animals. So are cats and
iguanas; but this is a dog page, not a cat and
iguana page.</P>

<HR>

<H2>The most popular dog breeds</H2>

<P>According to Sleeping Dogs, Inc. these are the
most <EM>popular</EM>dog breeds:</P>

<DL>
```

```
<DT><STRONG>Terriers</STRONG><DD>A small,
active breed of hunting dog.

<DT><STRONG>Retrievers</STRONG><DD>Any of
several breeds of dog that were trained to
retrieve game animals.

<DT><STRONG>Bulldogs</STRONG><DD>A short-
haired dog characterized by a large head,
strong jaw, and a thickset body.

<DT><STRONG>Collies</STRONG><DD>A large, agile
working dog originally developed in Scotland
as a sheepdog.

<DT><STRONG>Poodles</STRONG><DD>A non-sporting
dog with a dense coat which can be clipped in
a variety of styles.

</DL>

<HR>

<H3>My favorite dog</H3>

<P>My favorite dog is Herman, a silly looking
mutt with the body of a golden retriever and the
legs of a basset hound.</P>

<H3>Mom's favorite dog</H3>

<P>Mom's favorite dog is Sam, a sweet, hairy
little sheltie. Unfortunately, Sam is no longer
with us.</P>

</BODY>

</HTML>
```

2. Save the document.
3. In the browser, select **Reload** or **File, Open File** (or an equivalent command) to display the updated doghome.htm. Your screen should resemble Figure 29.

PRACTICE

Test your skills. See if you can change doghome.htm to look like the example in Figure 30! (*Hint:* Use <UL>, <DL>, <EM>, and <STRONG> tags.)

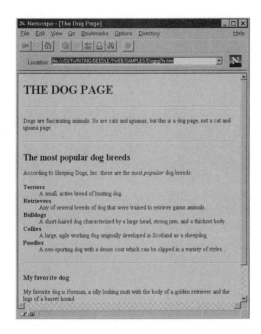

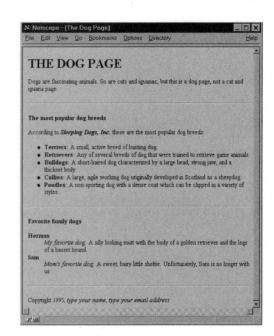

MORE HTML

In the following paragraphs you'll use line breaks, quotations, character entities, signature text blocks, preformatted text, and center tags in your HTML document.

LINE BREAKS

The line break <BR> tag breaks a line without creating a new paragraph at the location of the tag. The text wraps to the left margin of the current element. No extra space is added between the lines and no font changes take place. Line break characters can be used within any tagged items.

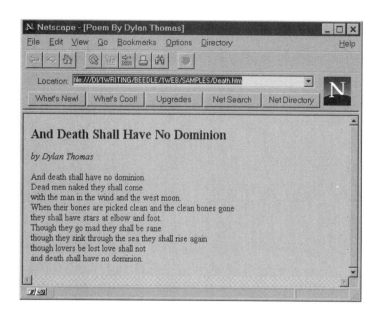

FIGURE 31   LINE BREAKS IN A POEM

The HTML for the poem shown in Figure 31 is as follows:

<H2>And Death Shall Have No Dominion</H2>

<P><I>by Dylan Thomas</I></P>

<P>And death shall have no dominion.

Dead men naked they shall come

with the man in the wind and the west moon.

When their bones are picked clean and the clean bones gone

they shall have stars at elbow and foot.

Though they go mad they shall be sane

though they sink through the sea they shall rise again

though lovers be lost love shall not

and death shall have no dominion.
</P>

Add the following horizontal line and short poem to doghome.htm.

1. In the HTML editor, type the following after the "Favorite Dogs" section.

    ```
    <HR>

    <H4>Poem written by a dog</H4>

    <P>Please give me that bone.<BR>

    Please give me that bone.<BR>

    Give me that bone.<BR>

    Give me that darn bone.</P>
    ```

2. Save the document.
3. In the browser, select **Reload** or **File, Open File** (or an equivalent command) to display the updated doghome.htm. Your screen should resemble Figure 32.

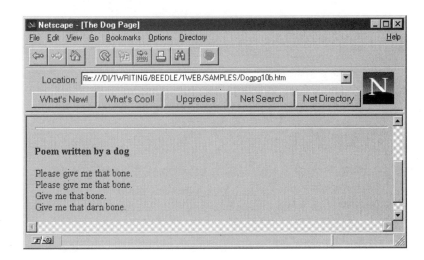

FIGURE 32   LINE BREAKS IN A DOG POEM

QUOTATIONS

A quotation is identified with blockquote `<BLOCKQUOTE>...</BLOCKQUOTE>` tags. Browsers display quotations in a variety of ways; some are indented or italicized, others are offset with blank lines. The format is as follows:

`<BLOCKQUOTE>`*quotation text*`</BLOCKQUOTE>`

Blockquotes can contain other tags and can themselves be inserted into lists as well as other blockquotes.

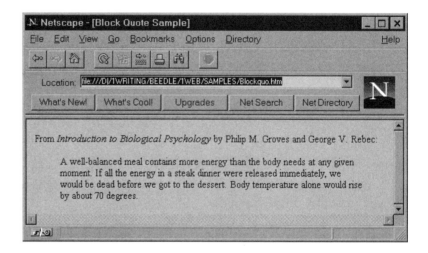

FIGURE 33   BLOCKQUOTE

The blockquote shown in Figure 33 is formatted in HTML as follows:

`<P><CITE>`From `<I>` Introduction to Biological Psychology `</I>` by Philip M. Groves and George V. Rebec:`</CITE></P>`

`<BLOCKQUOTE>`
A well-balanced meal contains more energy than the body needs at any given moment. If all the energy in a steak dinner were released immediately, we would be dead before we got to the dessert. Body temperature alone would rise by about 70 degrees.
`</BLOCKQUOTE>`

The `<CITE>` logical style tag isn't rendered distinctively in Netscape Navigator. In other browsers, however, it often is.

Reformat the dog poem in doghome.htm as a blockquote.

1. In the HTML editor, insert <BLOCKQUOTE> tags before and after the body of the poem. Remove the <P> tags and change the title of poem as follows:

    <HR>

    <BLOCKQUOTE>

    Please give me that bone.

    Please give me that bone.

    Give me that bone.

    Give me that darn bone.**
**

    <CITE>—Poem written by a dog</CITE>

    </BLOCKQUOTE>

2. Save the document.

3. In the browser, select **Reload** or **File, Open File** (or an equivalent command) to display the updated doghome.htm. Your screen should resemble Figure 34.

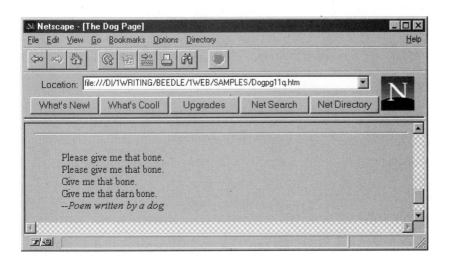

FIGURE 34   BLOCKQUOTE IN A DOG POEM

Four characters are reserved for use in HTML tags: left-angle bracket (**<**), right-angle bracket (**>**), ampersand (**&**), and double-quote mark (**"**). For these characters to be interpreted as text and not as tags, you must reference them as character entities.

John & Mary must be written as **John & Mary**

5 > 2 must be written as **5 > 2**

Character	Tag
>	&gt;
<	&lt;
&	&amp;
"	&quot;

CHARACTER ENTITIES

A character entity is a tag representing a special character such as the copyright symbol or the umlaut. Character entities can be inserted in any HTML text. Generally speaking, if a keyboard character requires more than pressing the Shift key to type it on screen (8-bit ASCII), it should be entered as a character entity. Sample character entities include the copyright symbol (©) and a double-quote mark ("). Note that the ampersand (&) and the semicolon (;) are essential components of character entities. You'll find a complete list of character entities in Appendix C.

Use caution with character entities because some browsers have trouble displaying them. Test your Web page on a variety of browsers to make sure the character entity is interpreted correctly.

PRACTICE

Reformat the quotation byline and signature line in doghome.htm as follows:

1. In the HTML editor, frame the blockquote with quotation marks (") and add a copyright symbol (©) as follows:

```
<HR>
<BLOCKQUOTE>
    &quot;Please give me that bone.<BR>
    Please give me that bone.<BR>
    Give me that bone.<BR>
    Give me that darn bone.&quot;<BR>
    <CITE>&#169; Bowser, 1995</CITE>
</BLOCKQUOTE>
<HR>
<P>&#169; 1995, <EM>type your name</EM>, <EM>type your e-mail address</EM></P>
```

2. Save the document.

3. In the browser, select **Reload** or **File**, **Open File** (or an equivalent command) to display the updated `doghome.htm`. Your screen should resemble Figure 35.

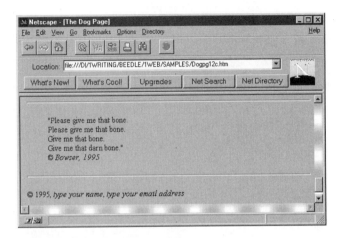

"Please give me that bone.
Please give me that bone.
Give me that bone.
Give me that darn bone."
© *Bowser, 1995*

© 1995, *type your name, type your email address*

FIGURE 35   CHARACTER ENTITIES IN A DOG POEM

SIGNATURE TEXT BLOCKS

Signature text blocks contain copyright information, lists of authors, update references, e-mail addresses and so on. They're typically placed at the bottom of a Web page, separated from the rest of the document by a horizontal rule <HR>. Tags associated with signature text blocks are <ADDRESS> and <A HREF="mailto:">. The <A HREF> tag is a hypertext link reference discussed in detail in the section on links.

Address tags <ADDRESS>...</ADDRESS> are used to denote signature blocks. They're usually formatted in italic, although some browsers add right justification. Addresses can include style tags, graphics, and links. The format is as follows:

```
<ADDRESS>address text</ADDRESS>
```

The `mailto:` addition is a link protocol used to send e-mail. When you click a `mailto:` link, the browser opens up a mail utility, allowing you to send e-mail to the individual addressed in the link. (More about links later in the book). If the browser doesn't support `mailto:`, it will display an error message. The `mailto:` format is as follows:

```
<A HREF="mailto:email address">email address</A>
```

Figure 36 shows a signature block with line breaks `<BR>`, a `mailto:` link, and style formatting `<STRONG>`.

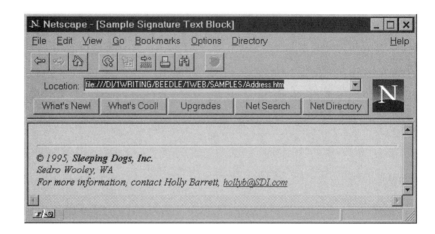

FIGURE 36 **SIGNATURE BLOCK**

The HTML for Figure 36 is as follows:

```
<HR>

<ADDRESS>&#169; 1995,<STRONG>Sleeping Dogs, Inc.
</STRONG><BR>

Sedro Wooley, WA<BR>

For more information, contact Holly  Barrett,
<A HREF="mailto:hollyb@SDI.com">hollyb@SDI.com</A>

</ADDRESS>
```

Reformat the signature text block at the bottom of `doghome.htm` as follows:

1. In the HTML editor, replace `<P>` with `<ADDRESS>` tags and include a `mailto:` link to your e-mail address as follows:

   `<HR>`

   `<ADDRESS>``&#169; 1995,` *`your name,`*

   `<A HREF="mailto:your email address">your email address</A></ADDRESS>`

   `</BODY>`

2. Save the document.

3. In the browser, select **Reload** or **File, Open File** (or an equivalent command) to display the updated `doghome.htm`. Your screen should resemble Figure 37.

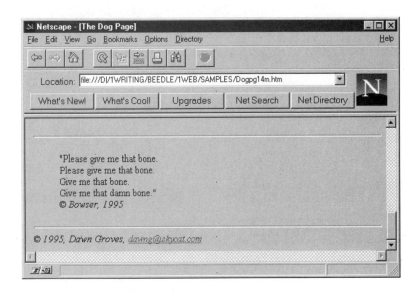

FIGURE 37   SIGNATURE BLOCK ON THE DOG PAGE

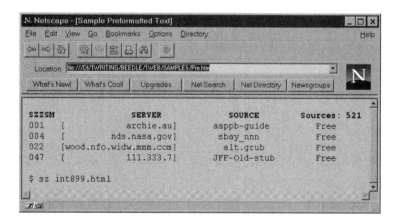

PREFORMATTED TEXT

Preformatted text uses a fixed-pitch font (often rendered as Courier) to preserve the spacing between letters and words. In HTML 2.0, this is the only way you can include white space in your text elements. Preformatted text is used to display tables, code, and any information that requires defined columns and spacing. (HTML 3.0 will support tables directly. See Appendix A.) Preformatted text is also used to maintain the spacing of entry fields for forms. (More on forms later in the book.) To preformat text, surround it with <PRE>...</PRE> tags. The format is as follows:

```
<PRE>text</PRE>
```

<PRE> text can include style tags, character entities and links. Because <PRE> doesn't format paragraphs, you can't include tags such as <P> or <ADDRESS> or headings. Use spaces, not tabs, to vertically align <PRE> text. Press Enter to start a new line.

FIGURE 38   PREFORMATTED TEXT

The HTML for Figure 38 is as follows:

```
<PRE>

<STRONG>SZZSM    SERVER    SOURCE   Sources: 521</STRONG>

001    [    archie.au]     aappb-guide              Free

004    [    nds.nasa.gov]    sbay_nnn               Free

022    [    wood.nfo.widw.mmm.com]    alt.grub  Free
```

```
047    [   111.333.7]        JFF-Old-stub     Free
$ sz int899.html
</PRE>
```

Add a short preformatted table of text to doghome.htm as follows. You'll need to switch back and forth between editor and browser as you add or subtract spaces to align the text.

1. In the HTML editor, add the following <PRE> table:

```
<HR>

<PRE>

<STRONG>      Price          Personality</STRONG>

Beeks         $2.00          Grumpy

Herman        $50.00         Friendly

Jackie        $36.72         Silly

</PRE>
```

2. Save the document.
3. In the browser, select **Reload** or **File, Open File** (or an equivalent command) to display the updated doghome.htm. Your screen should resemble Figure 39.

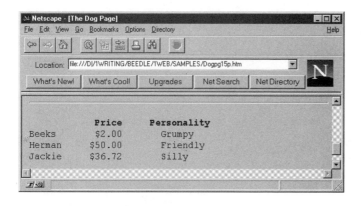

FIGURE 39   PREFORMATTED TEXT ON THE DOG PAGE

CENTERING

An interesting nonstandard Netscape alignment tag currently supported by many high-end browsers is <CENTER>...</CENTER>. This tag pair centers its contents relative to the width of the browser screen. The format is as follows:

```
<CENTER>text and tags</CENTER>
```

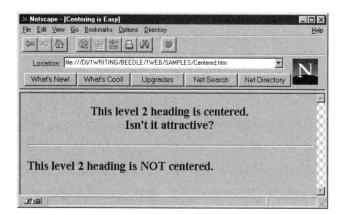

FIGURE 40   CENTERED TEXT

The HTML for Figure 40 is as follows:

<CENTER><H2>This level 2 heading is centered.

Isn't it attractive?</H2></CENTER>

<H2>This level 2 heading is NOT centered.</H2>

TRAVEL BY LINK

The easiest way to travel isn't by plane, train, or automobile—it's by link. Your only travel requirements are:

- A Web-connected computer
- A comfortable chair
- At least one of the five basic Web food groups: fat, salt, caffeine, sugar, megavitamins, and optionally, aspirin

A link is a word, phrase, or graphic that links the current document to another Web page, to another location within the same Web page, or to a graphic, sound, or video file. Links give the Web its dynamic character and appeal. They are visually distinct elements (also known as *hotspots*) that are colored and/or underlined. Graphic links are often bordered. When you click any part of a link, you download the file from the location dictated by the link's URL.

Links are typically found in menu-style lists; however, they can also be embedded in paragraph text. You've already explored some Web pages containing links. Here are a few sample screens to show you how links can be referenced.

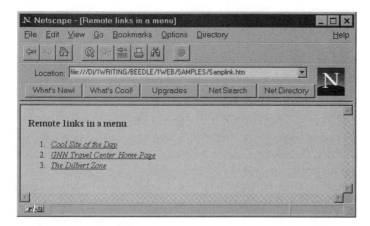

FIGURE 41   SAMPLE LINKS, MENU STYLE

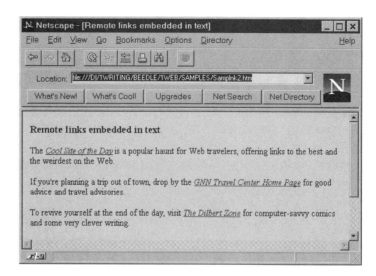

THE ANATOMY OF A LINK

In HTML, a link tag is designated by the tag pair `<A>link info</A>`. (Link tags are also known as *anchors;* hence the `<A>`.) Because links contain URLs and other associated information, they can often look complex and intimidating. However, when you understand the layout of a link, you'll find that it's a fairly simple construct with a few basic components. Figure 43 dissects the Cool Site of the Day link referenced in Figure 42.

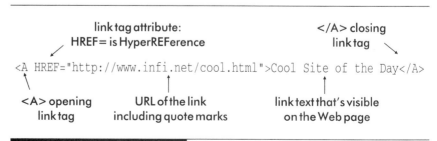

Notice:

- The <A> start tag contains a lot of information including a commonly used *attribute*, HREF=. (Attributes modify tags; unlike filenames, attributes are not case-sensitive.) This attribute stands for Hypertext REFerence, indicating that the text after the = is a URL. Another attribute you might see in the <A> tag is NAME=. We'll discuss NAME= later when we talk about links to a specific location on a Web page.

- The <A> start tag contains the URL of the file you want to see. The URL is enclosed in quotations with the closing angle bracket > immediately following the closing quotation marks. Note that the quote marks must be straight hash marks, not the more common typesetter quotes.

- Between <A> and </A> is the text that will serve as the virtual link, sometimes called the hotspot. This is what you'll see and click on the Web page.

- The </A> end tag closes the link.

- Links adopt the format of the element surrounding them. In other words, if the link is inside a <P> paragraph, it'll look like paragraph text. If it's inside an <H2> level 2 heading, it'll look like heading 2 text. See Figure 44.

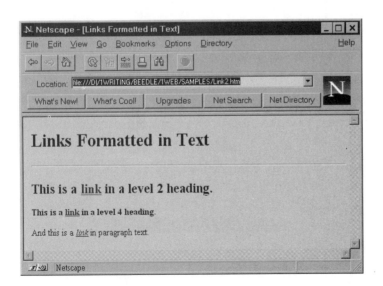

FIGURE 44   LINKS FORMATTED IN TEXT

RELATIVE VERSUS ABSOLUTE ADDRESSES

Links contain URLs embedded in the **<A>** tag. The URL is the address of the link. Addresses are divided into two groups: relative and absolute. The distinction between a relative and an absolute address rests in the location of the link's destination. All addresses must follow UNIX directory protocol.

RELATIVE ADDRESSES

A relative address describes the location of a file based on its relationship to the currently active Web page. Files addressed in relative terms are located on the same server, often in the same directory. Because the file is local relative to the active Web page, its address doesn't need to include the server name (domain). Even simpler, if the file is located in the same directory as the active page, the address doesn't even need a directory specified. When you reference files in your own Web site, you should use relative addressing because it requires little to no editing in case the directory is relocated.

To same directory:
<A HREF="*filename*">*visual hotspot*</A>

Example:
<A HREF="page2.html">Page 2</A>

(continued on next page)

FOUR SIMPLE LINKS

In this section we'll learn about four commonly used links:

- Links to an internal Web page
- Links to a specific location on the current Web page
- Links to a remote Web page
- Links to an image

We'll explore each of these links, the first three in this section and the fourth in the following section.

LINKS TO AN INTERNAL WEB PAGE

Most Web sites consist of links to more than one internal document. An internal document is stored on the server that contains your Web site, often in the same directory. The Blues Cafe included with this tutorial is an example of a local Web site that links to internal Web pages. Many personal Web sites include one or more internally linked documents such as a resume, a publicity photo, and an assortment of additional pages describing hobbies and haunts.

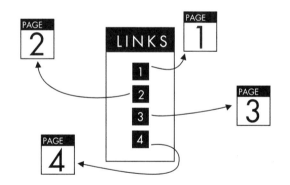

FIGURE 45   LINKS TO AN INTERNAL WEB PAGE

Internal files are easy to link because you can use relative addresses (see "Relative Versus Absolute Addresses"). If the linked pages are located in the same directory as your home page, you don't need to include the directory path. The format would be as follows:

```
<A HREF="filename">the text of the
hotspot</A>
```

PRACTICE

Let's give it a try. First you'll create a new HTML document, `terriers.htm`, with a internal link to `doghome.htm` and save it in the same directory as `doghome.htm`. Then you'll link `doghome.htm` back to `terriers.htm`. Ready?

1. In the HTML editor, create a new HTML document, `a:/terriers.htm`, as follows:

   <HTML>

   <HEAD>

   <TITLE>The Terrier Page</TITLE>

   </HEAD>

   <BODY>

   <H1>THE TERRIER PAGE</H1>

   <P>Sample page on terriers.</P>

   </BODY>

   </HTML>

   Hint: If you're using HotDog, click the New button 🗋 on the button bar or choose the **File, New** command. Replace the filler text in the `<TITLE>` and add the `<H1>` and `<P>` text.

2. Add a horizontal rule and a return link at the bottom of the page as follows:

   ```
   <P>Sample page on terriers.</P>
   ```

   <HR>

To parent directory:
<A HREF="../filename">visual hotspot</A>

Example:
<A HREF="../page2.html">Page 2</A>

To subordinate directory:
<A HREF="directory/filename">visual hotspot</A>

Example:
<A HREF="kitchen/page2.html">Page 2</A>

@ *Example:* Page 1 and Page 2 are both located in the **house** directory. If Page 1 is the active Web page, its **HREF=** link to Page 2 needs only to specify the filename, **<A HREF="page2.html">Page 2</A>**. With no directory included in the address, the browser will default to the current directory, **house**, on the current page's server.

@ *Example:* Page 1 is located in the **house** directory, and Page 2 is in the **house/kitchen** directory. If Page 1 is the active Web page, the link to Page 2 is **<A HREF="kitchen/page2.html">Page 2</A>**. The browser will look for **page2.html** in the **kitchen** directory, which is a subdirectory of the current directory **house**.

(continued on next page)

(continued on next page)

ABSOLUTE ADDRESSES

An absolute address includes the complete directory path from the top of the directory hierarchy through the directory tree ending at the Web page file. Absolute addresses look like the standard URLs you've come to know and love:

http://www.domain.com/ directory/filename.html.

An absolute address doesn't have to include the access method (**http://**) and domain name (**www.domain.com**) if the linked file is on the same server as the currently active Web page. Absolute addresses are typically used to link to remote files. If you use absolute addresses for your local Web site files, you'll end up editing them if the Web directory is relocated.

Different server:
<A HREF="http://domain/directory/filename">visual hotspot</A>

Example:
<A HREF="http://www.domain.com/ kitchen/ page2.html">Page 2 </A>

```
<A HREF="doghome.htm">Back to The Dog
Page</A>

</BODY>

</HTML>
```

Note: Remember, use only straight quotes, not typesetter quotes.

3. Save the document as `a:\terriers.htm`. (Be sure to save the file in the same directory as its home page, `a:\doghome.htm`.)

4. In the browser, if necessary, select **File, Open File** (or an equivalent command) to display `terriers.htm`. Your screen should resemble Figure 46.

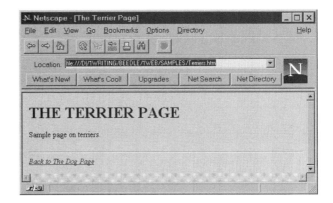

FIGURE 46   THE TERRIER PAGE

5. In the HTML editor, change the word `Terriers` in `doghome.htm` into a link to `terriers.htm`. If you've been doing the practices, your page will resemble the following. If it doesn't, just type the word "terriers" anywhere on `doghome.htm` and turn it into a link.

```
<P>According to Sleeping Dogs, Inc. these
are the most popular dog breeds:</P>

<UL>

    <LI><A HREF="terriers.htm">Terriers</A>

    <LI>Retrievers
```

```
<LI>Bulldogs
<LI>Collies
<LI>Poodles
</UL>
```

6. Save doghome.htm.

7. In the browser, select **File, Open File** (or an equivalent command) to display doghome.htm. If you click the **Back** button, be sure to click **Reload** as well. Your list should resemble Figure 47. (By this time, you've probably made a variety of changes to doghome.htm. Don't be concerned if the other elements on your page don't match this screen capture. The main thing is that the list contains the proper link and that the link works.)

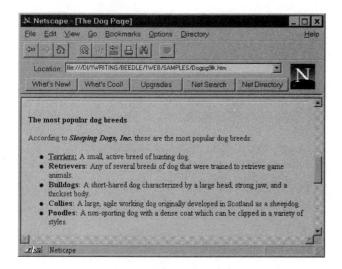

Same server:

<A HREF="/directory/ filename">visual hotspot </A>

Example:
<A HREF="/tierra/office/ cube/page2.html">Page 2 </A>

@ *Example:* Let's assume Page 1 and Page 2 are located on the same server. Page 1 is in the **/tierra/house** directory, and Page 2 is in the **/tierra/office/cube** directory. If Page 1 is the active Web page, the absolute link to Page 2 would be **<A HREF="/tierra/office/ cube/page2.html">Page 2</A>**. The browser will default to the current domain where Page 1 is located.

In this example, UNIX knows that it's an absolute address because the path starts with a forward slash (**/**).

8. Click the **Terriers** link to view The Terrier Page.

9. Click the **Back to The Dog Page** link to return to the home page.

LINKS TO A SPECIFIC LOCATION ON THE CURRENT WEB PAGE

On long or complicated Web pages, it's thoughtful to include internal links to portions of the document that aren't immediately visible. These links are generally found at the start of the page, enabling readers to quickly jump to the portion of the page they want to view. Links of this nature serve as a table of contents for the page. At the end of each section, a "Back" link (or a line of links) provide options to return to the top of the page or to continue reading. The Dog Link List page (Figure 48) is an example of this form of organization.

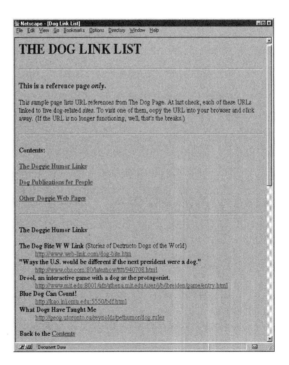

FIGURE 48   THE DOG LINK LIST

The View Source window shows:

```
<HTML>
<HEAD>
<TITLE>Dog Link List</TITLE>
</HEAD>
<BODY>
<H1>THE DOG LINK LIST</H1>
<HR>
<H3>This is a reference page <EM>only</EM> </H3>
<P>This sample page lists URL references from The Dog Page.  At last check, each of these URLs links
<HR>
<H4><A NAME="Contents">Contents:</A></H4>
<H4><A HREF="#Part 1">The Doggie Humor Links</A></H4>
<H4><A HREF="#Part 2">Dog Publications for People</A></H4>
<H4><A HREF="#Part 3">Other Doggie Web Pages</A></H4><HR>
<H4><A NAME="Part 1">The Doggie Humor Links</A></H4>
<DL>
<DT><STRONG>The Dog Bite W W Link</STRONG> (Stories of Destructo Dogs of the World)
<DD>http://www.web-link.com/dog-bite.htm
<DT><STRONG>"Ways the U.S. would be different if the next president were a dog "</STRONG>
<DD>http://www.cbs.com:80/lateshow/ttt/940708.html
<DT><STRONG>Drool, an interactive game with a dog as the protagonist </STRONG>
<DD>http://www.mit.edu:8001/afs/athena.mit.edu/user/j/b/jbreiden/game/entry.html
<DT><STRONG>Blue Dog Can Count!</STRONG>
<DD>http://fedida.ini.cmu.edu:5550/bdf.html
<DT><STRONG>What Dogs Have Taught Me</STRONG>
<DD>http://geog.utoronto.ca/reynolds/pethumor/dog.rules
</DL>
<H4>Back to the <A HREF="#Contents">Contents</A></H4>
<HR>
<H4><A NAME="Part 2">Dog Publications for People</A></H4>
```

FIGURE 49   THE DOG LINK LIST, DOCUMENT SOURCE

Another example: Let's say that you're authoring a sizey Web page describing tourist attractions around Seattle. You divide the Web page into three large sections: the waterfront, downtown, and the inland areas. At the top of the page, you list a table of contents describing the three sections to follow. The references in the table of contents are internal links to other parts of the same page.

Instead of a single link such as we created in the previous example, links to locations on the same Web page require a *pair* of links: The first link contains the HREF= attribute, essentially identifying your jumping-off point. The second link (called the *anchor*) contains the NAME= attribute, identifying your landing spot in the body of the document.

ⓘ The first link is the jumping-off point. Its format is as follows:

```
<A HREF="#destination">the text of hotspot</A>
```

The text after the pound sign (#) identifies the anchor you are jumping to. The text between the <A> and </A> identifies the visual hotspot that you

Links should be clearly listed, easy to find, and descriptive without being verbose.

1. Unless it's part of the style of your presentation, don't bury links in a lot of text. They should be easy to find, easy to understand, uncomplicated, and probably in a list if there are more than a couple of them.

Not as Good:

Snacks are important to me. First, I really like watermelons, and there's a great Web site about them. It's called **All About Watermelons**. Then there are cookies, a snack that's never out of style. **The Cookie Sheet** lists recipes and historical information about the most popular cookies in North America. But the best snack food is popcorn. Check out **The Popcorn Report** for details.

Good:

Web sites about my favorite snack foods:

All About Watermelons. (How to grow them, how to prepare them, new genetic strains)

The Cookie Sheet. (Recipes and useful crumbs of information)

The Popcorn Report. (The history and variety of popcorn, including a rating scale)

(continued on next page)

click. In The Dog Link List example, the first link is to The Doggie Humor Links.

@ The second link is the landing point, the *anchor.* Its format is as follows:

```
<A NAME="destination">the visible
anchor text</A>
```

Unlike the first link, the attribute is changed from HREF= to NAME= and there is no # in front of the destination text. Unlike other links, the anchor doesn't distinguish itself from the rest of the text by color or underlining. The anchor is the place you jump *to* when you click the hotspot identified by the HREF= link.

Using the Dog Link List as an example, note the HTML for the first half of the link pair (the jumping-off point), Dog Publications for People.

```
<A HREF="#Part 2">Dog Publications
for People</A>
```

By clicking this link, we jump to "Part 2" which looks like this:

```
<A NAME="Part 2">Dog Publications
for People</A>
```

You're jumping to the start of the section anchored as Part 2 with the visible text at the top of the screen, Dog Publications for People.

Links to a specific location are best practiced on long, complex Web pages. If you have time, feel free to add text to your practice Web page and insert your own internal location links.

LINKS TO A REMOTE WEB PAGE

The most common links are those to *remote* documents located on other servers. Most Web pages contain lists of interesting links to a variety of sites around the world. These links are very easy to format and are traditionally displayed in lists. All you need is the full, correct URL of the site you wish to reference. The format is as follows:

```
<A HREF="the URL to link
to">the text of the
hotspot</A>
```

An example of this is the link to the Cool Site of the Day in Figure 41. The HTML for that link is:

```
<A HREF="http://
www.infi.net/cool.html">Cool
Site of the Day</A>
```

Because this book isn't linking to anything but local files, you'll have to practice creating remote file links on your own. But as you can see, it's simply a matter of typing the full (absolute) URL instead of just the (relative) filename.

If you're already online, try adding this URL to your `doghome.htm` or `terriers.htm` page. Type the following:

```
<P>A great link that has
nothing to do with dogs is
the <A HREF=http://
www.infi.net/cool.html>Cool
Site of the Day</A></P>.
```

When you save the file and then reload it into the browser, click on the Cool Site of the Day link. The browser will then attempt to download the remote Web page.

WORKING WITH IMAGES

Images are the boon and the bane of the Web. As the boon, images add color, energy, and excitement to a Web page. As the bane, they slow down transmission time and are often unnecessary.

2. Make your link names descriptive. Link names are often used as database search keys by search engine robots. If your link doesn't clearly reference its subject matter, it's less likely to be found in a search.

Not as Good:

To **learn more** about watermelons, subscribe to the Melon Grower's Newsletter.

Good:

To learn more about watermelons, subscribe to the **Melon Grower's Newsletter**.

Not as Good:

Check out these helpful HTML authoring sites: **htmlhint.html htmletiq.html**

Good:

Check out these helpful HTML authoring sites: **General HTML Authoring Hints HTML Etiquette**

3. Resist the "click here" temptation. Telling readers to "click" is similar to recording a long-winded explanation on your answering machine about how to leave a message. Most people don't need answering machines reexplained for the umpteenth time. And the word "here" doesn't describe anything. (Also, for users who don't work with a mouse, the click reference is inappropriate.)

Not as Good:

To learn more about watermelons, click **here**.

Good:

To learn more about watermelons, subscribe to the **Melon Grower's Newsletter**.

Images come in two flavors: inline and external. Generally speaking, *inline* images download to your screen automatically. (Some browsers let you disable the automatic download.) *External* images are not automatically downloaded; you must click their associated links to initiate a download sequence and launch the necessary external *viewer program* (the program that interprets and displays the external image). Figure 50 contains an inline image and a link to an external image.

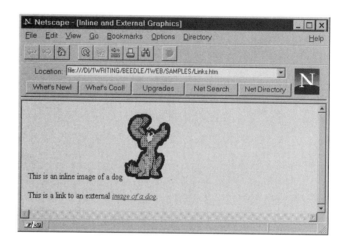

FIGURE 50   INLINE IMAGE AND A LINK TO AN EXTERNAL IMAGE

IMAGE FILE FORMATS

Common graphic file formats used on the Web are:

.gif   Currently, the most common inline image file format.
.jpeg, .jpg   Another commonly used image file format. Not all browsers can display inline JPEGs (Netscape Navigator does). JPEG format is a smaller file size than GIF and is best used for photo-quality images.

To convert a graphic into a GIF or JPEG format, use an editing program such as CorelDRAW or Adobe Photoshop.

Important:

- If you plan to use images that you haven't created yourself, make sure you get permission from the originator.

- Use repeat images for logos, return icons, and bullets, because they lend consistency to your Web pages. Repeat images also save time because no matter how often they're referenced, they need to be downloaded only once.

- Whenever possible, use relative addresses in your image links. Relative addresses prevent images from being downloaded a second time once they've already been viewed and cached. Absolute addresses cause the browser to download an image even though it's already cached.

INCLUDING INLINE IMAGES

Images can be embedded in almost any HTML element, or they can be placed in their own line of text. To include an inline image in your document use the <IMG> tag. The <IMG> tag includes three attributes: SRC= (mandatory), ALT=, and ALIGN= (both optional). Attributes aren't case-sensitive; <IMG SRC=> is equivalent to <IMG src=>.

SRC=   The filename of the image (mandatory).
       <IMG SRC="dog.gif">

ALT=   Alternative text for text-only browsers (optional). The brackets in the alternative text are a common convention but are not required. Also some browsers display the ALT= text before downloading the graphic.
       <IMG SRC="dog.gif" ALT="[Picture of a smiling dog]">

ALIGN= The alignment (top, middle, or bottom) of the image in relation to the baseline of the text string next to it (optional). In HTML 2.0, the ALIGN= attribute affects only the line containing the image. Other lines wrap above or below the graphic. HTML 3.0 provides attributes that wrap columns of text alongside of a graphic (ALIGN=left, ALIGN=right. See Appendix A.)
       <IMG SRC="dog.gif" ALT="[Picture of a smiling dog]" ALIGN=middle>

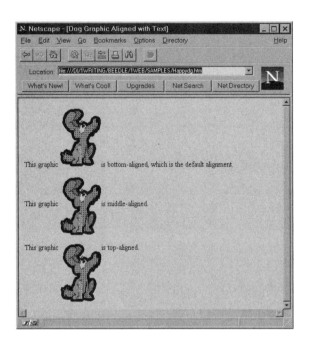

FIGURE 51   DOG GRAPHIC ALIGNED WITH TEXT

The HTML for the Figure 51 is as follows:

```
<BODY>

<P>This graphic <IMG SRC="happydg.gif" ALT="[smiling
dog,bottom-alignment]" ALIGN=bottom>is bottom-aligned,
which is the default alignment.</P>

<P>This graphic <IMG SRC="happydg.gif" ALT="[smiling
dog,middle-alignment]" ALIGN=middle>is middle-aligned.
</P>

<P>This graphic <IMG SRC="happydg.gif"ALT="[smiling
dog,top-alignment]" ALIGN=top>is top-aligned.</P>

</BODY>
```

INLINE IMAGES AS LINK ICONS

A small arrow icon or a similar graphic serves as an attractive, immediately recognizable link to a standard location such as a home page. To embed an inline image into a link, simply type the `<A HREF>` link as usual but insert the `<IMG SRC>` link between `<A HREF>` and `</A>`. The format is:

```
<A HREF="filename.htm"><IMG SRC="image_filename"></A>
```

If you want a text hotspot next to the graphic, the format is:

```
<A HREF="filename.htm"><IMG SRC="image_filename">visual hotspot</A>
```

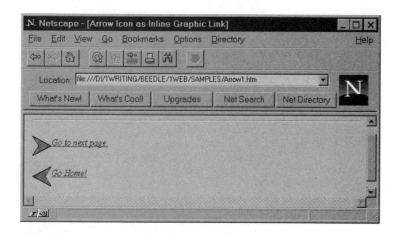

FIGURE 52   IMAGES AS NAVIGATION LINKS

Image links sometimes display borders around them in the same manner that text links are underlined. Stylistically, however, many Web authors choose to disable the border feature around image links in an effort to make them more attractive. Notice how the following HTML for the links shown in Figure 52 includes a `BOR-DER=0` attribute:

```
<BODY>

<HR>

<P><A HREF="nextpage.htm"><IMG SRC="arrow2.gif"
ALIGN=middle BORDER=0>Go to next page.</A></P>
```

TURN OFF THE IMAGE LINK BORDER

Many image links look much nicer without the standard link border surrounding them.

To hide the border, add a **BORDER=0** attribute to the **<IMG SRC>** tag as follows:

**<A HREF="*filename.htm*">
<IMG SRC="*image filename*"
BORDER=0> </A>**

For example:

**<A HREF="newpage.htm">
<IMG SRC="happydg.gif"
BORDER=0> </A>**

Some browsers ignore the **BORDER=0** attribute.

```
<P><A HREF="homepage.htm">
<IMG SRC="arrow.gif"ALIGN=middle
BORDER=0>Go Home!</A></P>

</BODY>
```

INLINE IMAGES AS BULLETS

A small image can sometimes be an interesting substitute for a standard browser-determined bullet character. Use restraint with this design technique, as even simple images can quickly overwhelm the text they're supposed to be emphasize. The format is

```
<IMG SRC="image.gif">text
```

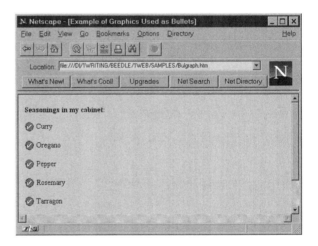

FIGURE 53   IMAGES AS BULLETS

The HTML for Figure 53 is as follows:

```
<P>Seasonings in my cabinet:</P>

<P><IMG SRC="bluedot.gif"
ALIGN=middle>Curry</P>

<P><IMG SRC="bluedot.gif"
ALIGN=middle>Oregano</P>

<P><IMG SRC="bluedot.gif"
```

```
ALIGN=middle>Pepper</P>

<P><IMG SRC="bluedot.gif" ALIGN=middle>Rosemary
</P>

<P><IMG SRC="bluedot.gif" ALIGN=middle>Tarragon</P>
```

Bullets can be inserted into almost any HTML element; however, they look best inside subordinate structures such as paragraphs <P>.

PRACTICE

Add an inline graphic to doghome.htm first as a separate element and then as part of a text string. Also add a home page inline icon to terriers.htm.

1. In the HTML editor, add the image as a separate element in doghome.htm.

   <IMG SRC="bigherm.gif" ALT="[a picture of Herman]">

   ```
   <H3>My favorite dog</H3>

   <P>My favorite dog is Herman, a silly looking
   mutt with the body of a golden retriever and the
   legs of a basset hound.</P>
   ```

   In the browser, the page should resemble Figure 54.

FIGURE 54   INLINE IMAGE AS SEPARATE ELEMENT

2. Move a small version of the image into the body text.

```
<H3>My favorite dog</H3>
```

```
<P>My favorite dog is Herman, <IMG
SRC="smalherm.gif" ALT="[a picture of Herman]"> a
silly looking mutt with the body of a golden
retriever and the legs of a basset hound.</P>
```

In the browser, the page should resemble Figure 55.

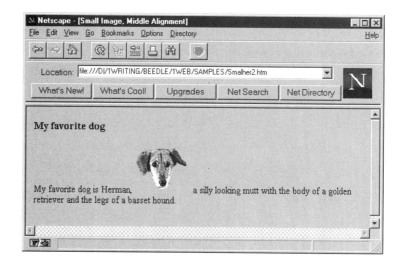

FIGURE 55   INLINE IMAGE IN BODY TEXT

3. Change the image alignment from default bottom to middle.

```
<H3>My favorite dog</H3>
```

```
<P>My favorite dog is Herman, <IMG
SRC="smalherm.gif" ALT="[a picture of Herman]"
ALIGN=middle> a silly looking mutt with the body
of a golden retriever and the legs of a basset
hound.</P>
```

The text is now aligned with the middle of Herman's ear instead of the base of his jaw. (Not all browsers support alignment options yet.)

4. Change the home page link on `a:/terriers.htm` into an `arrow.gif` icon.

```
<HTML>

<HEAD>

<TITLE>The Terrier Page</TITLE>

</HEAD>

<BODY>

<H1>THE TERRIER PAGE</H1>

<P>Sample page on terriers.</P>

<HR>

<A HREF="doghome.htm"><IMG SRC="arrow.gif"
ALIGN=middle BORDER=0>Back to The Dog Page</A>

</BODY>

</HTML>
```

In the browser, the page should resemble Figure 56. For fun, try removing the ALIGN= or BORDER= attributes to see how it changes the look of the link.

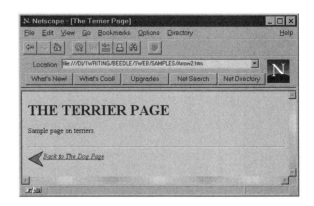

5. Click the link to make sure it works.

INCLUDING EXTERNAL IMAGES

An external image is linked to the Web page. You choose to download it by clicking the link. The link hotspot can be text or a *thumbnail* (smaller) version of the graphic. If the browser can't read the linked file format, it'll launch an associated viewer application. The viewer then displays the image. If the browser doesn't know the file type, it will ask if you want to save it to disk. The image won't appear onscreen.

Viewer applications handle more than image formats. Some viewers help you hear sound files or play video clips. (See the following section on multimedia.) Most browsers come bundled with one or more viewer applications which you can then configure. You can also download additional viewers as necessary. In Netscape Navigator choose **Options**, **Preferences**, then select the Helper Apps tab in the Preferences dialog box. The File type list shows the available viewers.

The format for an external image link uses the standard <A HREF> tag, but instead of linking to an HTML document, you link to an image file. The format is:

```
<A HREF="image_filename">visual hotspot</A>
```

If possible, external links should include adjacent text explaining the format and size of the file. This helps visitors decide whether to attempt the image download.

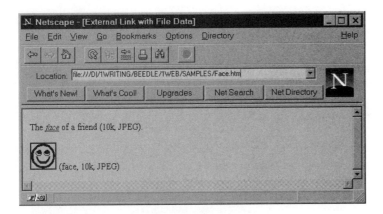

FIGURE 57   EXTERNAL IMAGE LINKS WITH FILE INFORMATION

The HTML for Figure 57 is as follows:

```
<BODY>

<P>The <A HREF="face.gif">face</A> of a friend (10k,
JPEG).</P>

<P><A HREF="face.gif"><IMG SRC="face.gif"></A>
(face, 10k, JPEG)</P>

</BODY>
```

INCLUDING MORE THAN ONE IMAGE

If you're using multiple images on one page, be sure that most of them are small and download quickly. If these images are repeating elements such as bullets or logos, use relative addresses. Relative addresses prevent time-consuming downloads because browsers cache recently used images in memory.

If you're listing multiple images, you may need to add a `<BR>` tag to prevent the images from displaying on the same line. For example, a single paragraph with no breaks at the end of each sentence would look like Figure 58.

FIGURE 58   DOG GRAPHICS WITHOUT BREAKS

PRACTICE

To doghome.htm, add an external graphic and then turn the text link into a thumbnail.

1. In the editor, add a link to bigherm.gif in doghome.htm.

    ```
    <H3>My favorite dog</H3>
    ```

    ```
    <P>My favorite dog is <A
    HREF="bigherm.gif">Herman</A>, a silly looking
    mutt with the body of a golden retriever and the
    legs of a basset hound.</P>
    ```

2. Save the document and then test the link to make sure it works. Click the Back button to return to doghome.htm.

3. In the editor, change the text link, Herman, into a thumbnail graphic link.

    ```
    <H3>My favorite dog</H3>
    ```

```
<P>My favorite dog is <A HREF="bigherm.gif"><IMG
SRC="smalherm.gif"></A>Herman<BR>,
```
a silly looking mutt with the body of a golden
retriever and the legs of a basset hound.</P>

4. Click the link to make sure it works. You should now have an image of Herman's head which links to a full body shot.

IMAGE TRANSPARENCY AND INTERLACING

Image transparency is created by selecting a pixel color (such as white) and using a utility program to render it transparent. For example, if the graphic has a white background, the white will disappear and the background of the browser screen will show through. Figure 59 shows an example.

FIGURE 59   IMAGE TRANSPARENCY

Transparency helps images blend with the browser screen, creating a more finished, professional look. Unfortunately, not all browsers can display transparent graphics. If this is the case, you can use an image-editing program to change the background pixels to a gray color similar to what you see on the browser screen. Ideally, the gray background will blend with the browser screen color creating the illusion of transparency (although not all browsers use gray as their window color!).

The best images to render transparent are those with distinct differences between the object and its background. Photographs don't lend themselves to transparency because of the dithering of colors. The background should be an even color, preferably one that isn't used in the body of the image. The latest shareware transparency utilities can be found on the HTML Writers Guild Home Page, `http://www.mindspring.com/guild/`. (See "Improve Your HTML Skills" in Appendix B.)

Interlaced inline graphics download as low-resolution files and then "fill in." They give you something to look at right away, becoming clearer as the download progresses. Because interlaced graphics provide immediate gratification, they can sometimes encourage impatient Web users to wait for the completion of the graphic download. Only GIFs can be interlaced (JPEGs cannot). The latest shareware interlacing utilities also can be found on the HTML Writers Guild Home Page.

IMAGE ADVICE

- If possible, use JPEGs for photo-quality graphics; GIFs are fine for all other images.
- Keep your images simple and small to reduce download time.
- Link big graphics instead of forcing the user to wait for them to download.
- Avoid including too many inline color images on a single page. It not only increases download time, it may also negatively affect the color quality of the art. (Many video cards run with 256 colors. If you include a lot of multicolored images on a single page, you may exhaust the available color palette entries. This forces the browser to approximate colors.)
- Use images only when they are truly necessary. Unnecessary images clutter up a screen and may increase download time.
- If appropriate, use thumbnails instead of big graphics to reduce download time.
- If appropriate, make your images transparent. This gives the Web page a more professional look.
- Consider interlacing large inline graphics. This gives users an immediate feel for the image before it's fully downloaded. It also lets them move to other Web pages if they're not interested in the graphic.

- Provide options for text-only browsers. Add ALT= text to your <IMG> tags. Consider adding parallel Web pages designed specifically for text-only browsers.

- Provide low-resolution and high-resolution graphics links. Let visitors choose which is most suitable for their browsers, monitors, and connection speeds.

- Include WIDTH=*pixel_width* and HEIGHT=*pixel_height* attributes in the <IMG> tag to generate a placeholder while the graphic downloads. This prevents the page from restructuring each time an image download is completed. Example: <IMG SRC="graphic.gif" WIDTH=100 HEIGHT=120>. Pixel dimensions must be accurate because the downloading graphic will resize itself to fit the specified placeholder.

- Use images that translate well into a variety of browsers and screen sizes. Keep in mind that not everyone is using the same browser setup as you.

ADVANCED TOPICS

This section briefly introduces multimedia files, imagemaps, and forms. (To learn about tables and backgrounds, see Appendix E.) Imagemaps and forms employ Common Gateway Interface (CGI) programs. These programs (sometimes called scripts) perform special or complex functions. Unlike the other simple HTML that you've learned, CGI scripts require learning more about the server on which your Web page will live. They also require that you learn to write CGI programs using a language such as C, Perl, or UNIX shell programming.

It isn't the intention of this book to teach you the details of CGI. Your Web page doesn't require them to be useful, attractive, and effective. However, as you become a more sophisticated Web page developer, you should take the time to learn how to write and use CGI scripts. Any of the references in Appendix B can provide details about CGI. For now, a simple introduction will do.

INTRODUCTION TO MULTIMEDIA

When it comes to the Web, multimedia usually refers to graphics, sound files, and video clips. Graphics were discussed in the previous section. Here we'll cover sound and video, both of which are handled in the same manner as external images. When the browser recognizes an attachment format, it launches a viewer program to "display" the data. If no viewer exists, the browser prompts you to save the file to disk.

Viewer applications exist in quantity for both audio and video files. Most online HTML reference sites contain links to shareware multimedia viewers.

WORKING WITH SOUND FILES

Sound files add musical clips, welcome messages, warning beeps, even background noises to your Web page. Typically, a sound file is indicated by a descriptive text link such as `Dog Barking` or a graphic link such as a picture of an ear, a musical notation, or some other evocative icon. Like images, sounds must be formatted appropriately to be interpreted by the browser. There are a variety of platform-specific formats including Macintosh `AIFF` (`dogbark.aiff`) and Windows `WAV` (`dogbark.wav`). The most common platform-independent file format is `AU` (`dogbark.au`). Platform-specific formats produce a better-quality sound than `AU`; however, they're obviously limited in terms of who can play them.

Sound file links are formatted similarly to image links, except that the file is sound data and not an image.

```
<A HREF="dogbark.au">Dog barking, 79k, AU</A>
```

Now hear this:

- ℗ Sound files can be generated at home with a proper microphone, sound card, and digitizing software. Sounds are also archived at various locations around the Internet and on CD-ROM. If you use someone else's sound file, make sure you have permission to do so.

- ℗ You must have a sound card installed on your computer to play sound files. Not everyone owns a sound card, which means that many people won't be able to play your sounds. The Web page should make sense without sounds.

- ℗ Sound files tend to be quite large. When you provide sound links on your Web page, be sure to list the file size and the format. To keep the size down, try recording sound bites in mono instead of stereo.

- ℗ Use an icon (such as an ear or a microphone) to indicate that a link is to a sound file. The format is:

```
<A HREF="dogbark.au"><IMG SRC="ear.gif">Dog bark-
ing, 79k, AU</A>
```

WORKING WITH VIDEO FILES

Video data adds "digitally encoded" motion video to your Web pages. Currently, the most common video format on the Web is MPEG (`movie.mpg`), however, Apple's QuickTime format (`movie.mov`) is gaining momentum. As with other external files, you must have a proper viewer application to play movie clips.

Video links are formatted similarly to image and sound links:

```
<A HREF="dogbark.mpg"> Dog barking, 1.5mb, MPEG</A>
```

Now see this:

- Video files can be generated at home with a properly configured computer. But your best bet is to locate video archives on the Net or purchase some royalty-free clips. As with all media files, if you borrow someone else's work, make sure you have permission.

- Not everyone can play videos, which means that many people won't be able to enjoy your video files. The Web page should make sense without them.

- Like sound files, video files tend to be quite large. Be sure to list the file size and the format next to the video link.

- Use an icon (such as an strip of film or a video camera) to indicate that a link is to a video. The format is:

```
<A HREF="dogbark.mpg"><IMG SRC="videocam.gif">Dog
barking, 1.5mb, MPEG</A>
```

INTRODUCTION TO IMAGEMAPS

An *imagemap* (also known as an active or "clickable" image) is a collection of links assigned to discrete parts of an inline image. A common example is a weather map of the United States. If you click California on the imagemap, you link to a regional weather page for California; if you click New Hampshire, you link to a regional weather page for New Hampshire.

Imagemaps require a graphical browser because of the inherent nature of the map; you must click a region of the image in order to access a link. Imagemaps are often used as navigation button bars and tables of contents. When the mouse is moved over the clickable area, the cursor turns into a hand.

Because each imagemap is different, this section will introduce you to the general features of clickable images and the necessary steps to build them. When you're ready to attempt an imagemap, consider reading more on the subject by searching the Web (see Appendix B for excellent online HTML resources).

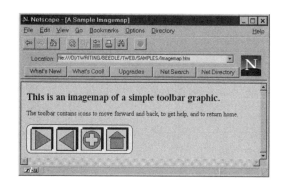

FIGURE 60   SAMPLE IMAGEMAP

A standard CGI program to process imagemap information is already written. This is good news, because the only things you have to provide are a suitable image, a map file, and the HTML to join them together.

PICKING A SUITABLE IMAGE

You need an image with distinctive regions or boundaries. A map is a classic example. Another example would be a picture of a refrigerator or a floor plan. Photographs or complex, multicolored images can be poor choices for imagemaps if their boundaries are unclear.

GENERATING A MAP FILE

A map file is literally a picture of the boundary areas you want defined. It's a simple text file written to run on the server; all you do is fill in the appropriate coordinates. In a map file the boundary areas of the image are defined by XY pixel coordinates. Each boundary area is then mapped to a specific URL. For example, the toolbar in Figure 60 contains four rectangular areas. When a defined area is clicked, the appropriate document is downloaded.

The easiest way to generate a map file is to use a map-editing utility such as mapedit (`http://sunsite.unc.edu/boutell/mapedit/mapedit.html`). The mapedit program generates the map file for you; all you have to do is click the mouse on the corners of the boundaries.

If you're generating the map file without a utility program, you'll need to type a standard map file program (described below), fill in the shape coordinates as appropriate, and then upload the program to the server. One way to determine shape coordinates is to import your image into a graphics program, locating the X and Y coordinates of each region by moving the cursor over the location and reading the numbers.

The two most popular servers (CERN and NCSA) recognize the following shape areas:

Point	The XY coordinates of the discrete point
Circle	The coordinates for a point at the center of the circle and the number of pixels in the radius
Rectangle	The coordinates for the upper-left and lower-right corners of the shape
Polygon	The coordinates for the point at each corner; the more points you identify, the more clearly you'll define the shape

The standard map file for a CERN server is formatted as follows:

```
default URL

circle (x,y) r URL

rectangle (x1,y1) (x2,y2) URL

polygon (x1,y1) (x2,y2) (x3,y3) ... (xn,yn) URL
```

The CERN map file for the toolbar in Figure 60 follows. Note that only rectangles are defined because no other shapes are used in the toolbar imagemap. Also note that # indicates a comment line.

```
#Outside of buttons, sorry

default http://servername/pathname/sorry.htm


#Button 1, go to next page

rectangle (10,6) (63,60) http://servername/
pathname/next.htm


#Button 2, go to previous page

rectangle (70,6) (123,60) http://servername/
pathname/previous.htm
```

```
#Button 3, go to help page

rectangle (130,6) (183,60) http://servername/
pathname/help.htm


#Button 4, go to home page

rectangle (190,6) (243,60) http://servername/
pathname/home.htm
```

The standard map file for an NCSA server is formatted as follows:

```
default URL

circle URL x,y r

rect URL x1,y1 x2,y2

poly URL x1,y1 x2,y2 x3,y3 ... xn,yn

point URL x,y
```

The NCSA map file for the toolbar in Figure 60 follows. Note that only rectangles are defined because no other shapes are used in the toolbar imagemap. Also note that # indicates a comment line.

```
#Outside of buttons, sorry

default http://servername/pathname/sorry.htm


#Button 1, go to next page

rect http://servername/pathname/next.htm 10,6
63,60


#Button 2, go to previous page

rect http://servername/pathname/previous.htm 70,6
123,60


#Button 3, go to help page

rect http://servername/pathname/help.htm 130,6
183,60
```

```
#Button 4, go to home page
rect http://servername/pathname/home.htm 190,6
243,60
```

In each case, URLs must be absolute; there are no relative pathnames in a map file. The order of appearance is important in a map file because if two regions overlap, the first region listed will supply the URL. The default URL (`sorry.htm`) is a fail-safe mechanism just in case you click outside the defined regions.

Map files are saved as `.map` in specific directories on the CERN or NCSA server. When you're ready to create a map file and save it, contact your server administrator to find the appropriate location to upload it.

BRINGING IT TOGETHER WITH HTML

To process imagemaps, your server must already have installed the appropriate imagemap CGI program. For CERN, this is `htimage`; for NCSA, this is `imagemap`. The HTML that joins together the CGI program on the server, the image file, and the map file you just created is:

CERN:

```
<A HREF="servername/filename/cgi-bin/htimage/
<path/mapname.map"><IMG SRC="image.gif" ISMAP>
</A>
```

NCSA:

```
<A HREF="servername/filename/cig-bin/imagemap/
<path/mapname.map"><IMG SRC="image.gif" ISMAP>
</A>
```

Type the preceding HTML link (CERN or NCSA as appropriate) into your document at the point that the imagemap is to be used. In both links, the `ISMAP` attribute tells the browser and server to send mouseclick coordinates to the CGI program for processing.

Important: Make sure your server has the most recent CGI imagemap software from CERN or NCSA. Check the CERN or NCSA Web sites for the latest versions or check with your server administrator.

INTRODUCTION TO FORMS

The HTML `<FORM>` element allows you to request specific data from Web page visitors. Using `<FORM>`, you can build fill-in forms that include option lists, radio buttons, check boxes, comment areas, and more. Forms don't process data; they merely provide a means by which data can be collected. As with other HTML elements, the form is fairly simple to design. Unlike other HTML elements, however, the form has no meaning without a server script to process its data. When the user indicates that the form is completed (usually by clicking a button), the data is transmitted to the server. A CGI script then processes the data, often by storing it in a database. Sometimes additional Web pages are built and downloaded to the client browser based on the input from the form. Common uses of forms include soliciting visitor input about a Web page, collecting vital statistics, or submitting messages to be distributed electronically.

Let's study a common style of form to better understand its components. This form generates a response page which confirms user input. The response page is shown in Figure 62. When you're ready to implement forms, be sure to check additional form tutorials available on many HTML resource sites.

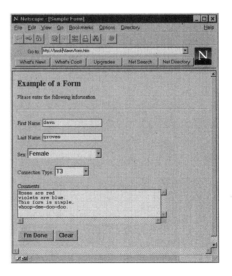

FIGURE 61   SAMPLE FORM ELEMENT

The HTML for the example in Figure 61 follows:

```
<HTML>

<HEAD>
```

```
<TITLE>Sample Form</TITLE>
</HEAD>
<BODY>
<H2>Example of a Form</H2>
<P>Please enter the following information.</P>
<!--form starts here-->
<FORM METHOD=POST ACTION="/cgi-bin/input_form">
<HR>
<P>First Name: <INPUT NAME="First" TYPE="TEXT"
SIZE=20>
<P>Last Name: <INPUT NAME="Last" TYPE="TEXT"
SIZE=20>
<P>Sex: <SELECT NAME="Sex">
  <OPTION>Female
  <OPTION>Male
  <OPTION>Male posing as Female
  <OPTION>Female posing as Male
  <OPTION>Other
  </SELECT>
<P>Connection Type: <SELECT NAME="Connection">
  <OPTION>T3
  <OPTION>T1
  <OPTION>ISDN
  <OPTION>28.8K
  <OPTION>14.4K
  <OPTION>9600
  <OPTION>Pathetic
  </SELECT>
<P>Comments:
<BR>
```

FORM ELEMENT ATTRIBUTES

The form in the example employs four common elements in the body: **<INPUT>**, **<SELECT>**, **<OP-TION>**, and **<TEXTAREA>**. There are many attributes that modify form elements. Those listed in the example are:

NAME

Assigns a variable name to data (mandatory). This identifies the item to the server-side script.

TYPE

Indicates what type of data to display on the form itself, such as a Checkbox or Radio button, a Reset button that resets the form to its default condition, a short **TEXT** line for simple text entries, a Submit button that sends the data to the server, and many others (optional).

VALUE

Assigns a default value to the element (optional).

```
<TEXTAREA NAME="Comments" ROWS=5
COLS=50></TEXTAREA>

<P><INPUT TYPE="submit" VALUE="I'm
Done"> <INPUT TYPE="reset"
VALUE="Clear">

</FORM>

<!--form ends here-->

</BODY>

</HTML>
```

The form element is identified by the tag pair <FORM>... </FORM>. The first line of the form indicates the server script that will receive and process the data.

```
<FORM METHOD=POST ACTION="/cgi-
bin/input_form">
```

In this case, the script is input_form located in the cgi-bin directory. The script and the form were written as a unit.

Within the start tag <FORM>, two attributes are listed: METHOD and ACTION. METHOD controls how form data is sent to the server. ACTION controls what happens to it when it gets there. In the preceding case, the METHOD is POST which parses (breaks) the data into separate elements as it sends it to the server. (The other METHOD option, GET, sends the data in a single long string.) The ACTION indicates that the input_form script receives and processes the data.

The next element tag is <INPUT>.

```
<P>First Name: <INPUT NAME="First" TYPE="TEXT"
SIZE=20>
```

The INPUT tag contains the attribute, NAME, assigning this data the variable name "First." The tag also includes a TYPE attribute, indicating that the field should be a TEXT 20 characters wide (SIZE). A similar INPUT tag follows with data for the "Last" variable.

The next element tag is `<SELECT>`.

```
<P>Sex: <SELECT NAME="Sex">

  <OPTION>Female

  <OPTION>Male

  <OPTION>Male posing as Female

  <OPTION>Female posing as male

  <OPTION>Other

  </SELECT>
```

The `<SELECT>...</SELECT>` tag pair functions in a manner similar to the lists you've already used (`<UL>` and `<OL>`). The difference is that the items in the `<SELECT>` list are pickable options `<OPTION>` instead of simple list items `<LI>`. Like the `<INPUT>` tag in the example, the starting `<SELECT>` tag also contains a `NAME=` attribute. (Other possible attributes include `SIZE=`, displaying a list box whose height is the specified SIZE value and/or `MULTIPLE`, indicating that more than one option can be selected.) Note that the list concludes with the `</SELECT>` end tag. A similar `<SELECT>` list follows.

The next form element is `<TEXTAREA>`.

```
<P>Comments:

<BR>

<TEXTAREA NAME="Comments" ROWS=5 COLS=50>
</TEXTAREA>
```

The `<TEXTAREA>...</TEXTAREA>` tags are freeform editing fields typically used for comments or any input not selected from a list. If in your HTML you include text between the open and closing `<TEXTAREA>` tags, it will appear inside the editing area as a default entry. The `NAME=` attribute identifies the variable field. It tells the CGI script what to call the information in the text area. The `ROWS=` and `COLS=` attributes describes the dimensions of the text area.

The final elements are `<INPUT>` tags that employ the `TYPE=` attribute.

```
<P><INPUT TYPE="SUBMIT" VALUE="I'm Done">
<INPUT TYPE="RESET" VALUE="Clear">
```

`TYPE="SUBMIT"` generates a Submit button. When selected, the Submit button delivers data to the server. This is required on all forms (unless you don't want the data sent to the server). `TYPE="RESET"` generates a Reset button. When selected, the Reset button resets the form field to their default values. This may not be a requirement, but it's certainly helpful to users who may want to adjust their entries.

The following is a sample CGI script written in Perl, used to process a form such as the example. The script takes the values in each fill-in text box and generates a simple HTML document which it sends back to the client for display. Many form-processing scripts also record the received values in databases for later reference.

CGI script:

```perl
#!/usr/bin/perl


print "Content-type: text/html\n\n";
print "<HTML><HEAD><TITLE>Sample script response</TITLE>
</HEAD><BODY>\n";
print "<H1>Response from sample form</H1>\n";


if ($ENV{'REQUEST_METHOD'} eq "POST") {

  $form = <STDIN>;        # get form data
  $form =~ s/\s//g; # remove whitespace
  $form =~        # convert escaped characters
      s/%([0-9a-f]{1,2})/pack(C,hex($1))/eig;
  $form =~ s/\+/ /g;
      # convert '+' characters back into spaces


  @entries = split(/&/, $form);
  # form fields are separated by '&' chars
  # create an array of the field/value pairs


  foreach $entry (@entries) {   # print out the field/value pairs
      ($item, $value) = split(/=/, $entry);
```

```
    print "<BR>The value of <B>$item</B> is <B>$value</B>\n";
    }
}
else {
  print "<P>Sorry, this script only supports the POST method\n";
}


print "</BODY></HTML>\n";
```

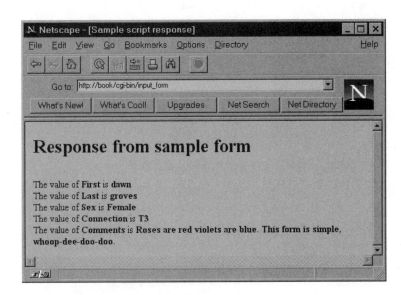

FORM RESTRICTIONS

As with other elements, forms have certain restrictions and idiosyncrasies.

    © Forms cannot be nested in headings, inside other forms, or between logical and physical style tags. They can, however, include embedded styles, headings, paragraphs, and lists.

- ⊘ Form elements align onscreen just as other elements do. To define the exact placement of the form items, surround the form contents with <PRE> tags. Use spaces to position the elements properly.

- ⊘ Not all browsers display forms equally. Some can't handle them at all. For this reason, you should develop a second version of your form appropriate to form-incompatible browsers. Add a link that allows users to download the form. Don't forget to include an e-mail address so they can send it back to you.

WHAT TO FIND OUT BEFORE CREATING A FORM

Bottom line: here's what you should do in order to implement forms:

- ⊘ Decide if you really need a form. Forms can be a turn-off to many Web users. Don't include a form just for the heck of it.

- ⊘ Investigate the capabilities of your server. Can it handle forms? If so, what are the particulars you need to know?

- ⊘ Study CGI scripting. You'll have to write a script to process the data received from your form. (See the example script and refer to Appendix B for further study.)

- ⊘ Study other forms. Notice that the best forms are simple, well organized, and require the least amount of typing.

DEVELOPING YOUR WEB PRESENTATION

A Web *presentation* describes everything about your Web site: its look and feel, the organization of pages and information, the flow. The bad news is that it's easy to create a bad or boring presentation; they proliferate the Web. The good news is that it's also fairly easy to create an interesting, even inventive presentation. All you need is some good advice and a little forethought. The good advice is supplied in the following pages. The forethought, well, that's up to you.

ORGANIZING THE STRUCTURE OF THE SITE

Before getting into the nuts-and-bolts development of your Web site, it's important to think about its overall organization. How will the pages relate to each other? Briefly, there are two ways to look at site organization: *hierarchical* (up and down) and/or *linear* (side to side). Most Web sites combine the two forms in a manner similar to Figure 63.

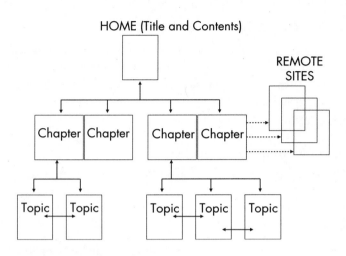

FIGURE 63   HIERARCHICAL AND LINEAR ORGANIZATION

Let's use a book metaphor to help visualize how these relationships can be organized. Think of the home page as the introduction and table of contents (links). From each item in the table of contents, you jump to a "chapter" page. Most chapter pages link to appropriate "topic" pages. Some topic pages may be linked to each other, forming linear relationships. Other topic pages may contain only links to remote Web sites. If your presentation is more complex, you can insert "section" pages between the home page and the chapter pages, or insert "subtopic" pages.

Like a book, your presentation can be "opened" arbitrarily from any page. You should provide descriptive links on each page, guiding visitors back to a logical chapter or home page. Unlike a book, each Web page should stand alone. Visitors shouldn't have to read other pages to make sense out of the site that they've entered. By making the <TITLE> descriptive of the contents as well as presentation (such as, "International Writers Consortium—Tips for Web Writers") and by including your address or home link at the bottom of each page, visitors can quickly orient themselves.

This is a simplified description of a typical Web presentation. There are many ways to organize them. The point is to keep the relationships among pages as uncomplicated and logical as possible. This will not only help visitors use your site, it'll also make it easier for you to maintain and upgrade it.

ORGANIZING THE INFORMATION ON A PAGE

In addition to thinking about the overall structure of the site, you must also think about the organization of information on individual pages and from topic to topic. Loose or sloppy organization generates a lack of confidence in the value of your presentation. If you want visitors to spend time at your site, the contents of each page should be orderly and navigable.

Four simple ways to organize information are:

- *Organize by location* (north, south, east, west; Mercury to Pluto). Destination sites and retail establishments often organize in this manner.

- *Organize by time* (first you do this, then this, then finally this). Sites that instruct typically structure their topics in this fashion.

- *Organize by comparative value* (most important to least important, expensive to inexpensive, old to new, fast to slow, complex to simple, most favorite to least favorite). This style can fit into almost any list of topics. There's usually some way to organize topics comparatively.

- *Organize alphanumerically* (A–Z, 1–9). This works on subjects with no geographic, time-specific, or comparative differences. Indexes are often organized in this manner, as are the white pages of the phone book. A simple alphanumeric sort makes it easy to locate topics.

Here's how you can use any of these four structures to organize a Web page about your favorite vacation spot, Seattle, Washington.

- *Seattle organized by location* (west to east—the waterfront, downtown, the inland areas). Topics (or links) in each of these locations might continue to be organized by place, or you could switch to comparative value.

- *Seattle organized by comparative value* (most-popular tourist attractions, secondary side trips, pleasant time-wasters). Topics (or links) in each of these areas could be organized by time or your personal merit-o-meter (i.e., Pappy's Picks, Endorsements by Eleanor).

- *Seattle organized by time* (visit Lake Washington for a morning jog, spend midday shopping downtown, and end the day with dinner at the Space Needle). Write about what to do first, second, and third in each of the destinations.

◎ *Seattle organized alphanumerically* (an alphabetical index of tourist attractions). Each item in the index is a link to the Web page that describes the attraction. An index of this sort would be best as a backup reference, not at the top of the presentation's hierarchy.

CONSTRUCTING YOUR PROTOTYPE

When you're developing something as potentially complex as a Web site, it's usually best to design and build a lean prototype. A prototype is a model, like an initial design or mockup. A prototype helps you get a handle on the size and scope of the project. It also provides direction for your efforts.

Think of your prototype development cycle as consisting of three simple stages: specification, design, and implementation. These are described in detail in this section. (Use the Web site development form on page 106 to record your ideas.)

DEFINING YOUR WEB SITE SPECIFICATIONS

Anybody can type text between a pair of <HTML>...</HTML> tags. As you browse the Web, you'll find many egocentric homilies with lots of words and little else. To create more than just another "This is me" stop on the Web, you must target your presentation appropriately and then design around your target ideas. To target your presentation, you must define a few important Web site specifications:

1. Decide the purpose of your Web page.

    Is it to advertise widgets? Is it to educate people about your nonprofit enterprise? Is it to tell a story? Is it to publicize you and your collected works?

2. Define your potential audience.

    The audience helps to guide your writing style, your inclusions, the approach you use, to publicize the site. Adults, teenagers, or children? Scuba divers? Gamers? Freelance writers? What are their personality traits? What are their interests? What do they want to see?

3. List the benefits people will receive by visiting your site.

    In the old days, just having a Web site was a big deal. Now most people require a good reason to visit your site. You must offer more than ego data. Benefits range from supplying entertainment (being an especially clever or weird spot), to demonstrating Web skills (an inventive use of graphics, forms, or whatever), to providing useful information. Think about your hobbies or your job. What information can you gather about a topic that is important to you? Practical information encourages repeat hits.

DESIGNING YOUR WEB SITE

Once you outline your Web specifications, you can use them to guide your Web site design process.

1. Describe the kinds of information to be presented at your site.

    Use the Web specifications to help guide your choices. In particular, consider the audience you want to attract. Brainstorm everything you'd like to include. Don't worry about the order of presentation, space considerations, or anything else.

2. Group subjects together.

    Think hierarchically. What subjects can be grouped under other subjects? Think about your home page and what you'd like as the table of contents. If some material seems too complicated to worry about right now, just leave it alone. You don't have to do everything.

3. Sketch a diagram of your site.

    Draw a rough flowchart. Use arrows to indicate link directions. (If all pages link to home, note it in your head; don't draw a million extra arrows.) If you don't know all your link pages or remote sites, don't worry about it. Remember that this design will develop over time.

4. Write a "to-do" list (optional).

    Based on the previous information, what do you need to find, do, or learn? Do you need to find appropriate graphics? Do you need to research a topic? Write a rough list of "to-do" items. Attempt to prioritize and, if possible, even date a few of them. If you have more than one task at the same priority level, do whatever is easiest or least expensive first.

5. Define a "stretch" task (optional).

    Think about something you might eventually add to your Web site that will stretch your HTML capabilities. This "stretch" is a guide for your studies. It'll help to broaden your Web authoring skills. If you're new to HTML, your stretch can be as simple as creating a thumbnail graphic. If you've got some HTML experience, your stretch can be adding an imagemap or creating a form.

IMPLEMENTING YOUR WEB DESIGN

With your specifications completed and your design roughly mapped out, it's time to get down to brass tacks. Time to start *writing*.

There a two simple ways to get going:

- ⊚ Start with the home page and work your way down through the links
- ⊚ Start with the individual "subject" pages and work your way up to the home page

The first method works well if you know what you want on your home page. The second method works well if you don't have a sense about the overall look of your presentation but you do know some detailed pages that you want to include. In any case, your end result probably won't look much like your original design. That's okay. It's all part of the physics of Web site development.

USING THE WEB SITE DEVELOPMENT FORM

The Web site development form guides you through the first two stages of Web site development: specification and design. Once you complete the form, you move into the implementation stage by beginning to construct a simple prototype of your site. It probably will need more work and time, but at least you'll be on your way.

Keep the following in mind as you go through the development process:

- ⊚ Don't get locked into perfection on any of this. Web pages *evolve*. When you're starting a new page or site, try for "okay " instead of "perfect."
- ⊚ Don't get rigid figuring out the details. Details can always be changed.
- ⊚ Fill out the form quickly. Keep moving through the questions. The faster you work, the less likely you'll become mired in a single idea or page concept. This is an overall envisioning process; you'll work out the details as you go along.
- ⊚ Have fun. This is a creative endeavor.

Take no more than 30 minutes to fill out this form. Enjoy the envisioning process but don't spend too much time on details. Don't worry if it's sketchy in places (you'll fill it in later). Once the time is up, begin authoring a simple local prototype of your home page or whatever page you choose to start authoring.

WEB SITE PROTOTYPE DEVELOPMENT FORM

SPECIFICATIONS (USE EXTRA PAPER IF YOU NEED MORE ROOM)

1. What is the purpose of your Web page?
   Example:

   > *The purpose of this Web page is to introduce me to the world. It's for fun, a job reference, and to advertise my writing.*

   Your turn:

2. Who is your audience?
   Example:

   > *Mostly adults. My preferred audience would be potential employers, friends of mine, vegetarians, people interested in my books. Potential employers would want to know about my work background, successes, professionalism. Friends would want to see the lighter side of me. Vegetarians would want support other Web sites on that subject. Maybe good recipes....*

   Your turn:

3. What benefits will people receive by visiting your site? If there's no benefit beyond reading about you and your life, think about your hobbies or your job. What information can you gather about a topic that is important to you? Practical information encourages repeat hits.
   Example:

   > *I'd like to include a list of Web sites on vegetarianism. Employers would want to see a good bio sketch and professional resume.*

   Your turn:

DESIGN

4. What kind of information will be presented at your site? (If you want to add information that doesn't cater to your audience, do you need to expand or change your audience specification?)

    Example:

    A welcome graphic; favorite links; pictures of my dog, Herman, and my family; a resume and brief bio sketch, a photo of me, a list of my heroes, my favorite music, my favorite vegetarian recipes, links to business associates.

    Your turn:

5. How can you group the subjects together?

    Example:

    Home page: welcome graphic, welcome text, menus of links, return address.

    Resume and Bio: all bio material including a photo of me, photos of my family, and, of course, Herman; maybe bio should be a link off resume.

    Vegetarian page: a link to veg pubs on the Net, recipe of the week, graphic of a happy chicken...

    Your turn:

6. How can you graphically sketch a diagram of your site? Use arrows to indicate link directions. Put question marks where you need to fill in data.

    Your turn:

7. Do you need to write a "to-do" list?

Example:

Design my prototype home page (today and tomorrow)

Design a welcome graphic   (next Saturday)

Convert my resume to HTML (date?)

Search the Web for veg sites (study about search utilities) (date?)

Your turn:

8. What do you want to eventually add that will stretch your HTML skills?

Example:

Add an audio file of Herman barking.

Your turn:

IMPLEMENTING YOUR WEB DESIGN

The implementation stage of Web site development is exciting and sometimes the most frustrating. This is when you put the pedal to the metal. Implementation not only involves actually writing the HTML, it also eventually involves getting your page(s) onto a server.

KEEPING YOUR WEB FILES ORGANIZED

If your Web presentation is uncomplicated (hopefully this is the case for your first site), save everything in the same directory. This makes it easy to upload files and maintain internal links. If your Web site is a complex array of icons, photos, and other elements, consider creating graphic and icon subdirectories. Remember that regardless of how you organize your files, always use relative addressing for internal links. (See "Relative Versus Absolute Addresses", pages 66–69.)

AUTHORING YOUR WEB PAGE

Are you ready? Let's get busy.

1. Quickly review the tutorial exercises at the front of the book. They'll remind you what you've already learned.

2. Create a Web directory for all your Web pages and graphics. Unless your site becomes complicated or overly large, save everything in the same directory. This simplifies your links as well as the transfer of the files to a Web server.

3. Start simple. Create the basic Web pages without detailed content.

4. Test each page in the browser as you create it. Save often. This makes it easier to catch mistakes.

5. Once you've created a home page and one or more topic pages, begin linking them.

6. Build on one or two pages at a time. Don't spread yourself too thin.

7. If you're in a classroom situation, be sure to save your page(s) on drive A so you can take them home.

8. Read Appendix B for details about uploading your site to an HTML server.

> **WHAT TO INCLUDE ON A HOME PAGE?**
>
> If you're not sure what to put on your home page, here's a quick list:
>
> - A title
>
> - A graphic image (could serve as the title)
>
> - A welcome paragraph, short and appropriate to your audience
>
> - A menu of links that clearly describes the contents of your Web presentation
>
> - A "footer" containing your address and a copyright statement

HELPFUL HINTS FOR STANDOUT WEB PAGES

Designing an effective Web presentation means learning and remembering a wide assortment of recommendations. The following lists categorize many of these seemingly unrelated bits of good advice, making them easier to reference and hopefully more likely to be implemented.

TO ENCOURAGE REPEAT VISITS

- Cater to what your audience wants and expects. If the audience is children, your writing style, layout, and graphics should be playful, bright, very easy to use, and energetic. If the audience is stockbrokers, your site should be solid, more formal, smart, and obviously well researched.

- Keep the links up to date and make sure your text is timely. This shows that you care about the site and that you'll keep it current.

- Include an update reference on appropriate pages (last updated: *date*). This tells visitors how current you really are.

- Clearly note what's new. This is characteristically accomplished on the home page by placing a link to the page(s) of new material. A small graphic often highlights the "What's New" link.

- Change your site periodically. Update information, add new links, and expand your format.

TO HELP VISITORS SCAN

- Make sure your information is logically organized.
- Maintain links in easy-to-reference menu lists.
- Make links as self-explanatory as possible.
- Include a home page (or high-level index page) link on almost every page.
- If your Web page is long:

  Include a table of internal links to help readers jump through the document.

  Make sure readers can jump back to the top of the page at the end of each logical section.

- Use horizontal rules (or graphics) to visually separate topic areas.
- Use the <TITLE> to identify the presentation as well as the content of the page.
- Make your page transitions as snappy as possible. Try not to weigh down the top levels of the presentation with time-consuming downloads.

TO ADD A PROFESSIONAL TOUCH

- Design your presentation around a theme and specialize in only a few topics. If you include too many unrelated topics, you'll seem like a dilettante and you won't inspire confidence in the quality of your information.

- Use small, tasteful graphics instead of browser-defined bullets and lines.

- Use repeating elements to create a unified look and feel on all your Web pages. For example, design a footer that includes your address, a small business logo, a home page link, and a horizontal rule. Use the footer consistently.

- Use icons as easily identifiable repeat links. For example, use repeating icons to identify the home, index, previous, and next pages.

- Use "express" links to help readers bypass introductory material. Help them get right to the heart of the presentation.
- Have someone else proofread your pages for typos. They'll catch the mistakes you can't see.
- Stay contemporary. When new HTML bells and whistles become widely available, implement them appropriately.
- Test your pages on at least two different browsers to be sure your pages are interpreted properly. If you employ a tag or feature that is browser-specific, be sure to inform users appropriately.
- Use HTML verification software (see the "Online Resources" section of Appendix B) to check the accuracy of your tags.

TO USE GRAPHICS MOST EFFECTIVELY

- Use thumbnail graphics as links to bigger graphics.
- If appropriate, make your graphics transparent and interlace them.
- Offer an alternative for text-only browsers. Include a text description of the graphic and, if appropriate, design duplicate pages without graphics. Offer visitors a link to either page.
- Don't include a graphic unless there's a specific need for it.
- Make sure the graphic clearly relates to the content of the page.
- Don't burden a page with too many graphics. It's annoying to wait for a bunch of graphics to download.
- Include descriptive size and file format information in ALT text. Example: `<IMG SRC="art.gif" ALT="Face.10K GIF">`.
- Include placeholder size attributes to prevent the Web page from resizing itself as graphics download. Example: `<IMG SRC="art.gif" WIDTH=100 HEIGHT=130>`.

ATTRACT VISITORS TO YOUR WEB SITE BY

- Publicizing the site to the your target audience, making sure that you highlight its special features.
- Registering your page with as many databases as possible.
- Making sure your Web page includes information that people will want to read.
- Listing your URL on all correspondence, published media, and e-mail.
- Including useful information at your site (a list of writer resource links, a gallery of free graphics or links to galleries of graphics, a frequently updated top-10 list of silly sites).
- Keeping your site up to date, easy to navigate, and interesting to view.

WEB-FRIENDLY WRITING

HTML authors sometimes forget that someone has to actually read their writing. It's easy to get so busy with structure that you lose sight of content. Here are a few general suggestions to make your digital prose inviting, succinct, and easy to understand.

- Keep paragraphs and sentences short. Long sentences tire and puzzle your readers. Average sentence length should be 10 to 14 words, less if you're writing a sales ad.

- Use short, simple words. Big words are supposed to impress people but they rarely do. If you are writing to communicate, use words that communicate easily.

- Be concise. Avoid vague antecedents.

  Bad: "It has been determined that the easiest way to . . ."

  Good: "The easiest way to . . ."

- Write in a friendly, conversational tone, talking to the reader by:
    - Using pronouns (I, we, you, they).
    - Using colloquial expressions on occasion (a sure thing, a rip-off, okay, and the like).
    - Using contractions (they're, you're, it's, here's, we've, I've).
    - Using simple words.
    - Using second person (you) instead of third person (the reader).
    - Varying sentence length.

      Example: "It's time we discussed conversational writing. Not the boring, jargon-filled stuff you read in trade journals. No, I'm talking about warm, simple words and sentences. The kind of writing Ann Landers does. (And she makes big bucks at it!)"

- Avoid clichés like the plague, especially the terms "*cool,*" "*surf,*" or "*information superhighway.*" They've been beaten into the ground.

- Keep adjectives to a minimum. Too many adjectives weaken the message and bloat the sentence. If possible, use verbs instead of adjectives and adverbs.

      Okay: He walked quickly across the street.

      Better: He dashed across the street.

      Okay: The asphalt was very hot.

      Better: The asphalt sizzled.

- Avoid sexist language. The days of the advertising man, stewardess, mailman, and fireman are over. Now we have the advertising professional, flight attendant, mail carrier, and fire fighter. To write nonsexist language, try the following:

  - Use plurals
  - Avoid reference to gender
  - Alternate gender references
  - Use "he and she" and "his and her" (avoid "he/she," "his/her")
  - Create an imaginary person

PROMOTING YOUR WEB PAGE

Good promotion is critical to increasing Web site traffic. Here are few suggestions to help galvanize your promotional efforts:

- *Tastefully* announce your page to the Internet; don't blast intrusive advertising hype into newsgroups around the world.

- Include your Web URL (and e-mail address) on all business stationery and correspondence.

- List your URL with every free Internet search engine, list, and catalog you can find. (Many good locations are listed below.) This may take you a few hours, but the increased visibility is well worth the time.

  Because many site administrators have backlogs of URLs to add, you may find a delay in getting listed. For this reason, some folks begin advertising their sites a few days to two weeks before they're actually ready. They put up placeholder pages with "under construction" notices. The only problem is that when users hit an "under construction" notice, they might not return when it's ready to go.

  Important: Carefully read each list's submission rules before posting your site.

- If you have an advertising budget, considering investing in a few high-traffic spots. Yahoo is a good example of an immensely popular Web site that charges for some (not all) of its promotional placement.

- Check Usenet and include appropriate announcements to targeted groups. (Make sure the group is amenable to the information you want to share; otherwise, you risk getting flamed.)

- Check local publications. Many newspapers and journals include weekly columns listing interesting new URLs.

- ◎ If you're a writer (and who isn't these days?), write articles for journals, newspapers, even e-zines and include your URL in the byline.

- ◎ If your site is especially interesting or unique, get someone to recommend it to Cool Site of the Day and other major traffic lists.

- ◎ If possible, monitor your site's traffic by checking access logs. This can be fairly complex, so check with your server administrator for details.

- ◎ The following are a variety of good locations for Web page promotion and announcements. (Remember, these URLs might be different by the time you're ready to promote yourself, and this list is by no means exhaustive—there are many more ways to get the word out than are listed here.)

  - **E-mail** an announcement to `net-happenings@is.internic.net` and `www-announce@info.cern.ch`.

  - **List with Yahoo,** a compendium of places dedicated to announcing you to the world (some free, some not): `http://www.yahoo.com/Computers_and_Internet/Internet/World_Wide_Web/Announcement_Services/`

  - **Directory of Directories,** maintained by Internic: For a small fee, you can post a limited entry. Send e-mail to `admin@ds.internic.net`.

  - **Submit it,** a (currently) free service that submits your URL to many major WWW catalogues. `http://www.submit-it.com/`.

  - **Web Launch,** a pricey but very high-traffic place to get noticed: `http://www.yahoo.com/docs/pr/launchform.html`.

  - **Open Market's Commercial Sites Index:** `http://www.directory.net/dir/submit.cgi`.

  - **New Internet Knowledge System,** noncommercial entries, e-mail: `javiani@rns.com`.

  - **WWW Virtual Library:** `http://www.org/hypertext/DataSources/bySubjet/Maintainers.html`.

  - **CERN's WWW Server List:** `http://www.org/hypertext/DataSources/WWW/Geographical_generation/new.html`.

  - **NCSA's What's New:** `http://www.ncsa.uiuc.edu/SDG/Software/Mosaic/Docs/whats-new-form.html`.

- **Netscape's What's New:** `http://home.netscape.com/escapes/submit_new.html`.
- Register with individual search databases:

   Lycos: `http://www.lycos.com/register.html`.
   ALIWEB: `http://web.nexor.co.uk/aliweb/aliweb.html`.
   WWW Worm: `http://wwww.cs.colorado.edu/wwww.html#new`.
   InfoSeek Corporation Server: `http://www.infoseek.com`. (If you think your site is cool, e-mail `cool@infoseek.com`.)
   WebCrawler: `http://webcrawler.com/WebCrawler/SubmitURLS.html`.
   Yahoo: `http://www.yahoo.com/`.
- **iMall Classified Ads,** insert a free classified ad: `http://www.imall.com/homepage.html`.
- **The Inter.Net,** a listing of home pages: `http://the-inter.net/cgi-bin/search.future`.
- **Galaxy Annotations:** `http://galaxy.einet.net/cgi-bin/annotate`.
- **The Hotlinks Guide:** `http://www.ilsi.com/`.
- **New Riders Yellow Pages:** `http://www.mcp.com/newriders/wwwyp/submit.html`.
- **Starting Point:** `http://www.stpt.com/util/submit.html`.

APPENDIX A
TABLE OF HTML TAGS

Tags are arranged alphabetically. Not all tags have been explored in this primer. Not all tags work in all browsers. Be sure to check that the tags you use display properly. To find out about the most recent tags, check the HTML Writers Guild Home Page `http://www.mindspring.com/guild/`.

<!-- ... -->

Definition:	Comment. Doesn't display onscreen. Keep each individual comment line fully contained within the tag pair. Don't use special characters (<, >, &, !) inside comment tags.
Attributes:	None.
Context:	Can be inside HTML.
Examples:	`<!--The start of the form.-->`
	`<!--Updated Nov 15, 1995.-->`

<A>...</A>

Definition:	Anchors for hypertext references. Contains either the destination (`NAME`) or the source (`HREF`) of the link.
Attributes:	`HREF="url of image"`: Mandatory. Web resource, FTP, TELNET, WAIS, e-mail, or gopher target location.
	`NAME="text"`: Optional. Target text within a document.
	`REL="next"` | `"previous"` | `"parent"` | `"made"`: Optional. Relationship between current anchor and destination. (Not supported by most browsers.)
	`TITLE="text"`: Optional. Title of destination document.

Context:	Can be inside ADDRESS, B, BLOCKQUOTE, BODY, CITE, CODE, DD, DT, EM, FORM, H1 through H6, I, KBD, LI, P, PRE, SAMP, STRONG, TT, and VAR.
	Can include B, BR, CITE, CODE, EM, H1 through H6, I, IMG, KBD, SAMP, STRONG, TT, and VAR.
Examples:	`<A HREF="http://dawng@skycat.com/images/` `widow.htm">The Web Widow</A>`
	`<A NAME="Part01">Part 1</A>`

\<ADDRESS>...\</ADDRESS>

Definition:	Electronic signature, author e-mail address. Typically placed at the bottom of documents. Usually rendered in italic.
Attributes:	None.
Context:	Can be inside BLOCKQUOTE, BODY, FORM.
	Can include A, B, BR, CITE, CODE, EM, I, IMG, KBD, P, SAMP, STRONG, TT, and VAR.

Example:	`<ADDRESS>Edgar Smith, 222 Elm Street,`
	`Bellingham, WA, 98227. Email:`
	`esmith@foo.com</ADDRESS>`

\<B>...\</B>

Definition:	Boldface text. Physical (hard) character format.
Attributes:	None.
Context:	Can be inside A, ADDRESS, B, BLOCKQUOTE, BODY, CITE, CODE, DD, DT, EM, FORM, H1 through H6, I, KBD, LI, P, PRE, SAMP, STRONG, TT, and VAR.
	Can include A, BR, CITE, CODE, EM, I, IMG, KBD, SAMP, STRONG, TT, and VAR.
Example:	`<P>My name is Bond, <B>James Bond</B>.</P>`

\<BASE>

Definition:	Document URL. Contains the complete URL upon which all internal URL references are based. If base isn't specified, browser uses current document URL. Optional.
Attributes:	`HREF="url"`.
Context:	Inside HEAD.

| Examples: | `<HEAD><BASE HREF="http://`
`dawng@www.skycat.com/file.html"></HEAD>` |

<BASEFONT>

Definition:	Specifies a basefont size for the entire document. (Netscape and Internet Explorer.) Relative <FONT> tags are determined according to this.
Attributes:	`SIZE="n"`. Optional. "N" is a size between 1 (smallest) and 7 (largest). Default is 3.
Context:	Can be inside BODY.
Examples:	`<BODY> <BASEFONT=4><FONT SIZE=+3>Go ahead,` `Make my day.</FONT>`

<BLOCKQUOTE>...</BLOCKQUOTE>

Definition:	Quotation. Often left-indented and/or offset from other text.
Attributes:	None.
Context:	Can be inside BLOCKQUOTE, BODY, DD, FORM, and LI. Can include A, ADDRESS, B, BLOCKQUOTE, BR, CITE, CODE, DIR, DL, EM, FORM, H1 through H6, HR, I, ISINDEX, IMG, KBD, MENU, OL, P, PRE, SAMP, STRONG, TT, UL, and VAR.
Example:	`< BLOCKQUOTE >...quoted text...</` `BLOCKQUOTE>`

<BODY>...</BODY>

Definition:	Document body. Contains the bulk of the document. Exclusive of the contents of HEAD.
Attributes:	`BACKGROUND="URL"` (*HTML 3.0,* for a tiled background graphic) `BGCOLOR="#$$$$$$"` (*Netscape,* for a background color, order in this and the following Netscape links is red/green/blue) `BODY TEXT="#$$$$$$"` (*Netscape,* for a text color) `BODY LINK="#$$$$$$"` (*Netscape,* for a link color) `BODY VLINK ="#$$$$$$"` (*Netscape,* for a visited link color) `BODY ALINK ="#$$$$$$"` (*Netscape,* for an active link)

Context:	Inside HTML.
	Can include A, ADDRESS, B, BR, BLOCKQUOTE, CITE, CODE, DIR, DL, EM, FORM, H1 through H6, HR, I, ISINDEX, IMG, KBD, MENU, OL, P, PRE, SAMP, STRONG, TT, UL, and VAR.
Example:	`<HTML><BODY>...body of document...</BODY></HTML>`
	`HTML><BODY BGCOLOR=#FFFFFF>...body of document...</BODY></HTML>`

`<BR>`

Definition:	A hard line break within an HTML element. Similar to a carriage return.
Attributes:	None.
Context:	Can be inside A, ADDRESS, B, BLOCKQUOTE, CITE, CODE, DD, DT, EM, FORM, H1 through H6, I, KBD, P, PRE, SAMP, STRONG, TT, and VAR.
Example:	`Roses are red `
	`Violets are blue `

`<CAPTION>...</CAPTION>`

Definition:	Table caption. Captions are horizontally centered above the table by default. Any HTML element used in a table cell can be used in a caption.
Attributes:	*Note that not all attributes work in all browsers. Check to make sure your browser can interpret them properly.*
	`ALIGN="above"` | `"below"` (Internet Explorer: `"left"` | `"right"` | `"center"`) Optional. Aligns caption above or below the table (on the left right or center of the line.)
	`VALIGN="top"` | `"middle"` |`"bottom"` | `"baseline"` Optional. Vertically aligns in the cell.
Context:	Can be inside TABLE.
	Can include any HTML element found in a standard HTML document.
Examples:	(A simple one row, three-column table with a 1-pixel border).

```
<TABLE BORDER=1>
<CAPTION>My Favorite Dogs</CAPTION>
<TR>
   <TD>Fred</TD>
   <TD>Marsha</TD>
   <TD>Bowser</TD>
</TR>
</TABLE>
```

<CENTER>...</CENTER>

Definition: An alignment tag that centers its contents relative to the browser screen width. (*Netscape*)

Attributes: None.

Context: Can be inside A, ADDRESS, B, BLOCKQUOTE, BODY, FORM, H1 through H6, I, P, and SAMP.

Can include A, ADDRESS, B, BLOCKQUOTE, BODY, CITE, CODE, DD, DT, EM, FORM, H1 through H6, I, IMG, KBD, LI, SAMP, STRONG, TT, and VAR.

Example: `<CENTER><H1>Hello World!</H1></CENTER>`

<CITE>...</CITE>

Definition: A citation of a publication or external resource. Logical (soft) character format. Often rendered in italic.

Attributes: None.

Context: Can be inside A, ADDRESS, B, BLOCKQUOTE, BODY, CITE, CODE, DD, DT, EM, FORM, H1 through H6, I, KBD, LI, P, PRE, SAMP, STRONG, TT, and VAR.

Can include A, ADDRESS, B, BLOCKQUOTE, BODY, CITE, CODE, DD, DT, EM, FORM, H1 through H6, I, KBD, LI, P, PRE, SAMP, STRONG, TT, and VAR.

Example:
```
<P>For more information, see
<CITE>Mustards of the World, Vol. 1
</CITE>.</P>
```

`<CODE>...</CODE>`

Definition:	Typed program code. Logical (soft) character format. Often rendered in a monospaced font. (Multiple lines of code should be formatted as PRE.)
Attributes:	None.
Context:	Can be inside A, ADDRESS, B, BLOCKQUOTE, BODY, CITE, CODE, DD, DT, EM, FORM, H1 through H6, I, KBD, LI, P, PRE, SAMP, STRONG, TT, and VAR.
	Can include A, B, BR, CITE, CODE, EM, I, IMG, KBD, SAMP, STRONG, TT, and VAR.
Example:	`<CODE>default /map/usa.html</CODE>`

`<DD>`

Definition:	Definition description. Part of a Definition list (DL).
Attributes:	None.
Context:	Can be inside only DL.
	Can include A, B, BLOCKQUOTE, BR, CITE, CODE, DIR, DL, EM, FORM, I, IMG, ISINDEX, KBD, MENU, OL, P, PRE, SAMP, STRONG, TT, UL, and VAR.
Examples:	

```
<DL COMPACT>
<DT>Ferrets
<DD>Low, long, busy, silly
<DT>Koalas
<DD>Squatty, sleepy, cute as the dickens
</DL>
```

`<DIR>...</DIR>`

Definition:	Directory list. Short items, no more than 20 characters. Some browsers displays the items across the screen in columns.
Attributes:	COMPACT (tighten line leading; not supported by all browsers).
Context:	Can be inside BLOCKQUOTE, BODY, DD, FORM, and LI.
	Can include LI.

Examples:
```
<DL COMPACT>
<LI>Part 1
<LI>Part 2
<LI>Part 3
</DL>
```

<DL>...</DL>

Definition: Definition list. Also known as a glossary list. Typically used when a term needs to be associated with a defining block of text.

Attributes: COMPACT (tighten line leading; not supported by all browsers).

Context: Can be inside BLOCKQUOTE, BODY, DD, FORM, and LI.

Can include DT and DD.

Examples:
```
<DL COMPACT>
<DT>Ferrets
<DD>Low, long, busy, silly
<DT>Koalas
<DD>Squatty, sleepy, cute as the dickens
</DL>
```

<DT>

Definition: Definition term. Part of a Definition list (DL).

Attributes: None.

Context: Can be inside only DL.

Can include A, B, BR, CITE, CODE, EM, I, IMG, KBD, SAMP, STRONG, TT, and VAR.

Examples:
```
<DL COMPACT>
<DT>Ferrets
<DD>Low, long, busy, silly
<DT>Koalas
<DD>Squatty, sleepy, cute as the dickens
</DL>
```

\<EM>...\</EM>

Definition:	Emphasized text. Logical (soft) character format. Often rendered as italic.
Attributes:	None.
Context:	Can be inside A, ADDRESS, B, BLOCKQUOTE, BODY, CITE, CODE, DD, DT, EM, FORM, H1 through H6, I, KBD, LI, P, PRE, SAMP, STRONG, TT, and VAR.
	Can include A, B, BR, CITE, CODE, EM, I, IMG, KBD, SAMP, STRONG, TT, and VAR.
Example:	`<P>Go ahead, <EM>Make my day.</EM></P>`

\<FONT>...\</FONT>

Definition:	Specifies a font size or color. (Netscape and Internet Explorer.)
Attributes:	COLOR="#rrggbb" | "colorname". Optional. SIZE="n" | "+n" | "-n". Optional. "N" is a size between 1 (smallest) and 7 (largest). A plus or minus in front of the number specifies a size relative to the BASEFONT setting.
Context:	Can be inside all common HTML structural elements. Can include all common HTML structural elements except the hierarchical \<H1>..\<H6> (typically, the \<FONT> tag is used in place of these elements) and \<TABLE> (the \<FONT> tag must be used in each table cell).
Example:	`<FONT SIZE=3>Go</FONT><FONT SIZE=+2>HOME!` `</FONT>`

\<H1>...\<H1> THROUGH \<H6>...\<H6>

Definition:	Header elements; six hierarchically ordered styles. Browsers determine appearance.
Attributes:	None.
Context:	Can be inside A, BLOCKQUOTE, BODY, and FORM.
	Can include A, B, BR, CITE, CODE, EM, IMG, KBD, SAMP, STRONG, TT, and VAR.

Examples:	`<H1>Top level heading</H1>`
	`<H2>Second level heading</H2>`
	`<H3>Third level heading</H3>`

< HEAD > ... </ HEAD >

Definition:	Document heading. Contains descriptive page information about the document. HEAD is not displayed in document text. If TITLE is specified, may appear in title window of browser. Exclusive of the contents of BODY.
Attributes:	None.
Context:	Can be inside only HTML. Can include BASE, ISINDEX, LINK, META, TITLE, and NEXTID. Must be inside HTML.
Examples:	`<HTML><HEAD>...</HEAD>...rest of docu-ment...</HTML>`

< HR >

Definition:	Horizontal rule.
Attributes:	None standard. (*Netscape optional:* `WIDTH="value"`, `LENGTH="pixels" | "percentage"`, `THICKNESS="pixels" | "percentage"`, `ALIGN="right" | "left" | "center"` and `NOSHADE` options.)
Context:	Can be inside BLOCKQUOTE, BODY, FORM, and <PRE>.

Example:	`<P> Text regarding subject 1.</P>`
	`<HR>`
	`<P> Text regarding subject 2.</P>`

< HTML > ... </ HTML >

Definition:	Document indicator. Contains the entire HTML document.
Attributes:	VERSION (currently, the default Document Type Definition (DTD) is `"-//IETF//DTD HTML//END//2.0"`).
Context:	Includes all HTML tags.
Example:	`<HTML>...entire html document...</HTML>`

< I > ... </ I >

Definition:	Italicized text. Physical (hard) character format.
Attributes:	None.
Context:	Can be inside A, ADDRESS, B, BLOCKQUOTE, BODY, CITE, CODE, DD, DT, EM, FORM, H1 through H6, I, KBD, LI, P, PRE, SAMP, STRONG, TT, and VAR.

Can include A, B, BR, CITE, CODE, EM, IMG, KBD, SAMP, STRONG, TT, and VAR.

Example: `<P>His name was <I>Angus McGee</I>.</P>`

<IMG>

Definition: Inline images.

Attributes: `SRC="url of image"`: Mandatory

`ALIGN="top" | "middle" | "bottom"`: Optional. Aligns graphic with baseline of text. Not supported by all browsers. (*Netscape:* `absmiddle`, `baseline`, `absbottom`.)

Other attributes not supported by all browsers:
`WIDTH="pixels"`,
`HEIGHT="pixels"`, `BORDER="pixels"`,
`VSPACE="pixels"`, `HSPACE="pixels, HEIGHT ="pixels"`.
`ALT="alternative text for non-graphic browsers"`. Optional.
`ISMAP`: Used with imagemaps. Optional.

Context: Can be inside A, ADDRESS, B, BLOCKQUOTE, CITE, CODE, DD, DT, EM, FORM, H1 through H6, I, KBD, LI, P, SAMP, STRONG, TT, and VAR.

Examples: `<IMG SRC="images/webwidow.gif" ALIGN="middle" ALT="Info on the Web Widow">`
`<A HREF="http://dawng@skycat.com/images/ widow.htm"> <IMG SRC="webwidow.gif" ALT="Thumbnail of Web Widow"> </A>`

<ISINDEX>

Definition: Document supports CGI scripts for searches. Optional.

Attributes: None.

Context: Inside HEAD. (Older documents sometimes show it in BODY, BLOCKQUOTE, DD, FORM, and LI.)

Example: `<HEAD><ISINDEX><TITLE>...document title...</TITLE></HEAD>`

<KBD>...</KBD>

Definition:	Keyboard input. Logical (soft) character format. Often rendered in a monospaced font.
Attributes:	None.
Context:	Can be inside A, ADDRESS, B, BLOCKQUOTE, BODY, CITE, CODE, DD, DT, EM, FORM, H1 through H6, I, LI, P, PRE, SAMP, STRONG, TT, and VAR.
	Can include A, B, BR, CITE, CODE, EM, I, IMG, SAMP, STRONG, TT, and VAR.
Example:	`<P>Press the <KBD>ENTER</KBD> key.</P>`

<LI>

Definition:	List item. Belongs to any of the list styles.
Attributes:	None.
Context:	Can be inside DIR, MENU, OL, and UL. (Some browsers allow character formatting inside LI.)

Examples:	`<OL COMPACT>`
	`<LI>Wet the dog.`
	`<LI>Soap the dog.`
	`<LI>Rinse the dog.`
	`</OL>`

<LINK>

Definition:	Describes relationship between this document and other documents or URLs. Points to a related document, an index, or next or previous documents. Ideally used to preload documents, although few browsers have this capability. Optional. Rarely used.
Attributes:	Same as Anchor tags <A>.
Context:	Inside HEAD.
Example:	`<HEAD><LINK HREF="nextdoc.html"><TITLE>...document title...</TITLE></HEAD>`

<MENU>...</MENU>

Definition: Menu list. Often with tighter leading than other list types.

Attributes: COMPACT (tighten line leading; not supported by all browsers)

Context: Can be inside BLOCKQUOTE, BODY, DD, FORM, and LI.
Can include LI.

Example:
```
<MENU COMPACT>
<LI>Forms
<LI>Image Maps
<LI>Tables
</MENU>
```

<META>

Definition: Describes other information about the document content.
Used for indexing. Optional. Rarely used.

Attributes: CONTENT: Value for a named property.
NAME: Names the property (title, author, date, and so on).
HTTTP-EQUIV: Binds META to a response header from the
server.

Context: Inside HEAD.

Example:
```
<HEAD><META NAME="doc.html"
CONTENT="firstdoc"><TITLE>...document
title...</TITLE></HEAD>
```

<NEXTID>

Definition: A unique numeric identifier generated by text-editing software,
used to describe the next document. Allows HTML documents
to be chained together. Optional.

Attributes: None.

Context: Inside HEAD.

Example:
```
<HEAD><NEXTID="N=55"> <TITLE>...document
title...</TITLE></HEAD>
```

<OL>...</OL>

Definition: Ordered (numbered) list.

Attributes: COMPACT (tighten line leading; not supported by all browsers).

Context:	Can be inside BLOCKQUOTE, BODY, DD, FORM, and LI. Can include LI.
| Example: | ```
<OL COMPACT>
<LI>Wet the dog.
<LI>Soap the dog.
<LI>Rinse the dog.
</OL>
``` |

<P>...</P>

Definition:	Paragraph text, typically rendered with extra space above the <P>. (*Note:* Currently, the end tag </P> is not mandatory; however, it may be necessary in future versions of HTML. In some browsers, use of the end tag </P> adds a little extra space between paragraphs.)
Attributes:	None standard. (*Netscape optional:* ALIGN="center" | "left" | "right" | "justify" | "indent".
Context:	Can be inside ADDRESS, BLOCKQUOTE, BODY, DD, FORM, and LI. Can include A, B, BR, CITE, CODE, EM, I, IMG, KBD, SAMP, STRONG, TT, and VAR.
| Examples: | ```
<P>Work becomes a stage, a playground for
awareness and generosity of spirit. Work
no longer defines you, it's simply another
way to express yourself.</P>
<P>Compassion gives meaning to your life
and purpose to your daily actions. Every
situation becomes an opportunity to live
with a deeper, more profound sense of
satisfaction.</P>
``` |

<PRE>...</PRE>

Definition:	Preformatted text. Useful for preserving the spacing and line breaks of tables, code listings, and text. Usually rendered in monospaced font. Use spaces, not tabs, to vertically align text.
Attributes:	WIDTH="nr": Optional. Specifies number of characters in a line. Often ignored by browsers.
Context:	Can be inside ADDRESS, BLOCKQUOTE, BODY, DD, FORM, and LI.

Can include A, B, CITE, CODE, EM, I, HR, KBD, SAMP, STRONG, TT, and VAR.

Example:
```
<PRE>
NAME        FAVORITE FOOD      E-MAIL ADDRESS
Dawn        Watermelon         dawng@skycat.com
Pappy       Steak              pappy@home.com
John        Latte              jg@onandoff.org
Bob         Candy bars         bobg@NDSU.edu
Phil        Oregano            philg@UCSD.edu
Eleanor     Guava jelly        eleanor@home.com
</PRE>
```

\<SAMP\>...\</SAMP\>

Definition: Sequences of literal characters. Usually rendered in monospaced font.

Attributes: None.

Context: Can be inside A, ADDRESS, B, BLOCKQUOTE, BODY, CITE, CODE, DD, DT, EM, FORM, H1 through H6, I, KBD, LI, P, PRE, SAMP, STRONG, TT, and VAR.
Can include A, B, BR, CITE, CODE, EM, I, IMG, KBD, SAMP, STRONG, TT, and VAR.

Example:
```
<P>The search returned the following zip
codes:</P>
<SAMP>
98226<BR>
90210<BR>
92910<BR>
</SAMP>
```

\<STRONG\>...\</STRONG\>

Definition: Strong emphasis. Logical (soft) character format. Often rendered as boldface text.

Attributes: None.

Context: Can be inside A, ADDRESS, B, BLOCKQUOTE, BODY, CITE, CODE, DD, DT, EM, FORM, H1 through H6, I, KBD, LI, P, PRE, SAMP, STRONG, TT, and VAR.

Can include A, B, BR, CITE, CODE, EM, I, IMG, KBD, SAMP, STRONG, TT, and VAR.

Example: `<P>Remember to <STRONG>pay your dues </STRONG>.</P>`

<TABLE>...</TABLE>

Definition: Container tag pair for an HTML table.

Attributes: *Note that not all attributes work in all browsers. Check to make sure your browser can interpret them properly.*

BORDER="pixels". Optional. Defaults to zero, meaning that no border will be drawn around the table.

CELLSPACING="pixels". Optional. The space inserted between individual table cells. (Netscape defaults to CELLSPACING=2.)

CELLPADDING="pixels". Optional. The space between the individual cell border and its contents. (Netscape defaults to CELLPADDING=0.)

WIDTH="pixels" | "percent". Optional. Defines absolute or percent-of-page table width. When used in TH and TD tags, describes the width of the cell.

ALIGN="left" | "right". Internet Explorer 2.0 Optional. Aligns table on the left or right of the page, allowing text to wrap around it.

VALIGN="top" | "middle" | "bottom" | "baseline" Optional. Vertically aligns text at the top or the bottom of the cell.

Context: Can be inside ADDRESS, BLOCKQUOTE, BODY, DD, H1 through H6, LI, P.

Can include <TH>, <TR>, <TD>

Examples: (A simple one row, three-column table with a one-pixel border.)

```
<TABLE BORDER=1>
<TR>
     <TD>Fred</TD>
     <TD>Marsha</TD>
     <TD>Bowser</TD>
</TR>
</TABLE>
```

\<TD>...\</TD>

Definition: Table cell data. Can contain any of the standard HTML elements normally present in an HTML document. Default alignment is ALIGN=left and VALIGN=middle.

Attributes: *Note that not all attributes work in all browsers. Check to make sure your browser can interpret them properly. Alignment attributes specified in TR are overridden by those specified in TD.*

COLSPAN="value". Optional. The number of columns this cell should span. Default is 1.

ROWSPAN="value". Optional. The number of rows this cell should span. Default is 1.

ALIGN="left" | "right" | "center". Optional. Aligns the cell data inside the cell.

VALIGN="top" | "middle"" | "bottom" | "baseline". Optional. Vertically aligns in the cell.

Context: Can be inside TR.

Can include any standard HTML structural element.

Examples: (A simple one row, three-column table with a one-pixel border).

```
<TABLE BORDER=1>
<TR>
        <TD>Fred</TD>
        <TD>Marsha</TD>
        <TD>Bowser</TD>
</TR>
</TABLE>
```

<TH>...</TH>

Definition: Table header. Header cells are boldfaced with a default center alignment.

Attributes: *Note that not all attributes work in all browsers. Check to make sure your browser can interpret them properly.*

COLSPAN="value". Optional. The number of columns this cell should span. Default is 1.

ROWSPAN="value". Optional. The number of rows this cell should span. Default is 1.

ALIGN="left" | "right" | "center". Optional. Aligns the cell data inside the cell.

VALIGN="top" | "middle" | "bottom" | "baseline". Optional. Vertically aligns in the cell.

Context: Can be inside TR.

Can include any standard HTML structural element.

Examples:

```
<TABLE>
<TR>
<TH COLSPAN=3>Dogs</TH>
</TR>
...table data
</TABLE>
```

<TITLE>...</TITLE>

Definition: Document title. Titles should succinctly describe the contents of the document. Not displayed in document text. May appear in title window of browser.

Attributes: None.

Context: Inside HEAD. Text only; no hypertext.

Example: `<HEAD><TITLE>...This is my document title...</TITLE></HEAD>`

<TR>...</TR>

Definition: Table row designation. When specified, ALIGN and VALIGN attributes become defaults for all cells in the row.

Attributes: *Note that not all attributes work in all browsers. Check to make sure your browser can interpret them properly. Alignment attributes specified in TR are overridden by those specified in TD.*

ALIGN="left" | "right" | "center". Optional.
Aligns cell text on the left, right, or center of the cell within the
row.

VALIGN="top" | "middle" | "bottom" |
"baseline". Optional. Vertically aligns text in the cell
within the row.

Context: Can be inside TABLE.

Can include TD, TH.

Examples: (A simple one row, three-column table with a one-pixel
border).

```
<TABLE BORDER=1>
<TR>
      <TD>Fred</TD>
      <TD>Marsha</TD>
      <TD>Bowser</TD>
</TR>
</TABLE>
```

<TT>...</TT>

Definition: Keyboard input. Physical (hard) character format. Often
rendered in a monospaced font.

Attributes: None.

Context: Can be inside A, ADDRESS, B, BLOCKQUOTE, BODY, CITE,
CODE, DD, DT, EM, FORM, H1 through H6, I, KBD, LI, P, PRE,
SAMP, STRONG, TT, and VAR.

Can include A, B, BR, CITE, CODE, EM, I, IMG, SAMP,
STRONG, TT, and VAR.

Example: `<P>Type <TT>RUN PTM.EXE</TT>.</P>`

<UL>...</UL>

Definition: Unordered (bulleted) list.

Attributes: COMPACT (tighten line leading; not supported by all browsers).

Context: Can be inside BLOCKQUOTE, BODY, DD, FORM, and LI.
Can include LI.

Examples:	`<UL COMPACT>`
	`<LI>Oranges`
	`<LI>Apples`
	`<LI>Watermelons`
	`</UL>`

<VAR>...</VAR>

Definition:	Highlights a placeholder variable meant to be supplied by the user. Logical (soft) character format. Usually rendered in italic or bold italic.
Attributes:	None.
Context:	Can be inside A, ADDRESS, B, BLOCKQUOTE, BODY, CITE, CODE, DD, DT, EM, FORM, H1 through H6, I, KBD, LI, P, PRE, SAMP, STRONG, TT, and VAR.
	Can include A, B, BR, CITE, CODE, EM, I, IMG, SAMP, STRONG, TT, and VAR.
Example:	`<P>Type <KBD>http://source.com/`
	`<VAR>filename.htm</VAR></KBD>` in the space
	`provided.</P>`

FORMS TAGS

The following tags are used in the definition of forms. Not all browsers support forms. This is a brief overview of these tags; further study is necessary. See "Online Resources" in Appendix B.

<FORM>...</FORM>

Definition:	Fill-in forms. (Not all browsers support forms.)
Attributes:	ACTION= "URL": Mandatory. Where form content is sent when Submit button is selected.
	METHOD= "GET" or "POST": Optional. Tells browser how to send information to the server at the ACTION URL. If METHOD isn't specified, GET is the default. GET appends the form's data to the current page URL. POST sends the form contents as a message block, allowing for more information to be transferred in a cleaner fashion.
	ENCTYPE= "MIME type": Optional. Specifies format of submitted data for the POST method. Default is application/x-www-form-urlencoded.

Context: Can be inside BLOCKQUOTE, BODY, DD, and LI.
Can include A, ADDRESS, B, BLOCKQUOTE, CITE, CODE,
DIR, DL, EM, H1 through H6, HR, I, IMG, INPUT,
ISINDEX, KBD, MENU, OL, P, PRE, SAMP, SELECT, STRONG,
TEXTAREA, TT, UL, and VAR.

Example:

```
<HTML>

<HEAD>

<TITLE>Sample Form</TITLE>

</HEAD>

<BODY>

<H2>Examples of a Form</H2>

<P>Please enter the following information.

<!--form starts here-->

<FORM METHOD="POST" ACTION="cgi-bin/input_form">

<HR>

<P>First Name: <INPUT NAME="First" TYPE="TEXT"
SIZE=14 MAXLENGTH=20>

<P>Last Name: <INPUT NAME="Last" TYPE="TEXT"  SIZE=14
MAXLENGTH=20>

<P>Street: <INPUT NAME="Street" TYPE="TEXT" SIZE=30
MAXLENGTH=40>

<P>City: <INPUT NAME="City" TYPE="TEXT" SIZE=14
MAXLENGTH=20>

<P>State: <INPUT NAME="Street" TYPE="TEXT" SIZE=2
MAXLENGTH=2> ZIP: <INPUT NAME="Zip" TYPE="TEXT"
SIZE=10 MAXLENGTH=10>

<P>Sex: <SELECT NAME="Sex">

     <OPTION>Female

     <OPTION>Male

     </SELECT>

<P><INPUT TYPE="submit" VALUE="Submit"> <INPUT
```

```
TYPE="reset" VALUE="Clear">

</FORM>

<!--form ends here-->

</BODY>

</HTML>
```

<INPUT>

Definition: Input object on form. Note that BLOCKQUOTE, P, and list elements can be used to organize input objects inside FORM.

Attributes: TYPE="text" | "password" | "checkbox" | "hidden" | "radio" | "submit" | "reset": Mandatory. The type of input element. *Text:* single-line text entry field. *Password:* prompts for password. *Checkbox:* On/off checkbox, default off. *Hidden:* data is not seen by the user. *Radio:* On/off radio buttons grouped by NAME. *Submit:* button that sends data to the server. *Reset:* button that clears data from the form.

NAME="variable name": Mandatory. The name of the INPUT element.

ALIGN="top" | "middle" | "bottom": Optional. Aligns element with baseline of text

CHECKED: Valid only with TYPE="checkbox" | "radio".

MAXLENGTH="nr": Length of text box. Optional.

SIZE="nr": Size of INPUT field.

SRC="URL"=: Mandatory with TYPE="image".

VALUE="value": Mandatory with TYPE="radio".

Context: Can be inside only FORM and any element inside FORM.

<OPTION>...</OPTION>

Definition: Options available inside <SELECT>...</SELECT>. Users must select a value from a list of options. End tag </OPTION> is not required.

Attributes: VALUE="value": Optional. Text string for the option.

SELECTED: Optional. Selects a default value in case the user doesn't make a choice.

DISABLED: Optional with some browsers. Marks option as disabled, gray or faded on onscreen.

Context: Can be inside SELECT.

<SELECT>...</SELECT>

Definition: Select one or more options from a list. Each alternative is tagged OPTION.

Attributes: MULTIPLE: Optional. Choose more than one option.

NAME="name": Mandatory. Variable name associated with the SELECT element.

SIZE="nr": Optional. Number of displayed text lines. Default is 1 (displayed as pull-down menu.) If value >1, list is often a scroll box.

Context: Can be inside only FORM.

Can include OPTION.

<TEXTAREA>...</TEXTAREA>

Definition: A text input area used to enter more than one line of text. Typically handles unlimited amounts of text. Scroll bars let users enter more text than the area can visibly contain.

Attributes: NAME="name": Mandatory. The name of TEXTAREA contents.

COLS="nr": Optional. Width of text area in columns.

ROWS="nr": Optional. Height of text area in rows.

Context: Can be inside only FORM.

APPENDIX B
WHERE TO GO FROM HERE

GETTING IT UP AND OUT

The following steps will help you move from your "local Web" to the Internet.

1. Shop for a service provider that will let you up upload your Web page(s) and maintain them. The most common issues to consider include disk space (how big your site is), traffic, and extra features such as forms processing and imagemaps (some providers won't allow you access to their cgi-bin directory). Talk to your provider about the best way to upload your data to their system. If you can't find a local provider to rent you Web space, send an e-mail message to LISTPROC@EINET.NET with "GET INET-MARKETING WWW-SVC-PROVIDERS" in the body of the message.

2. Find out what kind of server you're uploading to. If the server is UNIX, and your files and links all have three-character .htm extensions, you'll need to rename them with .html extensions (once they're uploaded). If the server is on a PC, you may not need to rename the filename extensions.

   UNIX is case-sensitive, which means that you must be sure to use the same upper-/lowercase lettering in your Web document's associated link references as you used in its filename.

   Note: Typically, you rename uploaded files via FTP or TELNET. You'll need to talk to your service provider about how best to accomplish this.

3. In HotDog, "publish" your files once you're ready to upload them. Do this by selecting the **Publish Document** command from the **File** menu. This option will ready the current pages for uploading to the Internet. The pub-

lished document filename extension changes from `.htm` to `.pub` to distinguish it from other files and to remind you that it'll need to be changed to `.html` when uploaded to the server.

By publishing your documents, you include server-specific conversions and enhancements as selected in **Publishing Options** (**Tools** menu, **Options** command, **Publishing** tab). Publishing Options let you save final Web documents to a separate directory, convert DOS backslashes (\) into UNIX forward slashes (/), and so on. Read more about publishing documents in HotDog's Help.

IMPROVING YOUR HTML SKILLS

HTML is constantly developing and expanding. To stay on the cutting edge of Web page design, you must continue to improve your skills and keep abreast of new developments. Fortunately, this is fairly easy to do. Make weekly Web visits to the best development and design information sources. A few suggestions are as follows:

- **The HTML Writers Guild Home Page.** From this source you can find almost any HTML-related information you're seeking. This includes online tutorials, supportive articles, Web page development software (browsers, editors, translators, converters), HTML newsgroups for sharing ideas and asking questions, HTML software and book reviews, and much more: `http://www.mindspring.com/guild`.

- **webreference. com.** An excellent site containing all the best web development links. Easy to use and navigate. `http://www.webreference.com`.

- **Dave Siegel's Home Page.** An extravaganza of blasphemous Web page design advice coupled with gorgeous examples and down-to-earth workarounds. Well worth studying but you need table-friendly Netscape Navigator to appreciate it: `http://www.dsiegel.com`.

- **Word.** When you want to see just how wild Web pages can be (and you have a fast connection), take your table-friendly browser to `http://www.word.com/index.html`.

OTHER USEFUL HTML RESOURCES

BOOKS

When it comes to learning a new program or a programming language, it helps to have more than one reference book. Different authors present the same information in a variety of useful ways. If you're serious about developing your HTML skills, consider investing in one or more of the following books. (No doubt many more fine works will be available when this book is published.)

Teach Yourself Web Publishing with HTML in a Week, Laura Lemay (Indianapolis, IN: Sams Publishing, 1995)
An easy tutorial and reference organized on a day by day basis. Simple, humorous, and thorough. Good for beginners.

The HTML Sourcebook: A Complete Guide to HTML, Ian S. Graham (New York, NY: John Wiley & Sons, Inc., 1995)
A well-written manual that explains complex concepts in a simple manner.

HTML for Fun and Profit by Mary E. S. Morris
A no-nonsense, detailed, clearly written description of HTML. An excellent resource book for serious HTML developers.

The World Wide Web Unleashed by John December and Neil Randall (Indianapolis, IN: Sams Publishing, 1994)
An in-depth description of the Internet and the Web. Of particular interest is the focus on "Web Weaving" with plenty of design methodologies and examples. This book does a fine job describing how to approach Web presentation design projects on a professional level.

HTML for Dummies, Ed Tittel & Steve James (Foster City, CA: IDG Books, 1995)
A fairly detailed description of HTML in an easily accessible language and style.

ONLINE RESOURCES

Keep in mind, URLs are always changing. If you can't find the resource by typing in the URL, look for an alternative resource. There are many.

- **Forms generation:** `http://www2.ncsu.edu/bae/people/faculty/walker/hotlist/forms.html`
- **HTML translators and converters:** `http://www.utexas.edu/learn/pub/transed.html`
- **The Web Developers Virtual Library,** useful HTML and Web development information: `http://www.stars.com:80`

- **The Docs's WebDev Page,** ditto above: `http://www.webcom.com/~docline/webdev.shtml`
- **WWW Consortium,** the folks "in charge." `http://www.w3.org`

CONFESSIONS OF AN HTML HERETIC

After reading this book, you no doubt appreciate that a good Web page favors content quality and multiplatform structure over layout control. If this is true, then why do so many sites:

- Emphasize layout?
- Use background colors and graphics even though these features are ignored by many browsers?
- Use tables to control line size even though tables aren't part of the current standard and can't display on many browsers?
- Advise you to view their material using only specific browsers?

Web site authors often choose to do any or all of the above because, contrary to HTML philosophy (here comes the heresy), layout *is* important—not as important as content, but still important. The Web is a visual medium much like television. It has an internal light source that shines through the monitor screen, generating strong images and bright colors. These images and colors are pretty to look at but often arduous to read for an extended length of time. To make Web pages more readable, you often must take issue with HTML default layout and make some changes.

- **Limit line size.**

  A line of over 10 words is more difficult to read than a shorter line. Line breaks can be controlled by inserting `<BR>` tags or by using tables. (See Appendix F.)

- **Change the background color and/or texture to something gentle on the eye.**

  Changing backgrounds is a feature that many high-end browsers support. Ideally, the background should be soft, providing a clear differentiation between text and screen color. (See Appendix F.)

- **Increase the font size.**

  Changing fonts and font sizes and is supported by only a few browsers. HTML lets you control font size by tag assignment. That is, `<H1>` tags traditionally display larger fonts that <H2> tags. As browsers become more sophisticated and HTML matures, font control will no doubt become standardized. Note that in Netscape Navigator, you can specify a default display font size from the **Options** menu, Preferences dialog box.

@ **Shorten the verbiage (see "Web-Friendly Writing").**

Regardless of your layout, you should always tighten and polish your text. This makes an enormous difference in readability and doesn't involve HTML in the least.

As HTML matures, these and many other sexy options will no doubt become standardized. Until then, HTML heretics will preach their layout philosophies, dictating which browser best displays their wares.

Bottom line: Don't get caught up in layout until you're sure that your content is good. Content is by far the most important component of a good Web site. Everything else is icing.

TABLE OF SPECIAL CHARACTERS AND CHARACTER ENTITIES

◎ This table represents only the most common character symbols.

◎ Not all special characters have both character entities and numeric entities. Blank spaces are not errors.

Character Symbol	Numeric Entity	Description	Character Entity
	&$32	Space	
!	&#33;	Exclamation point	
"	&#34;	Double quotation	&quot;
#	&#35;	Number sign	
$	&#36;	Dollar sign	
%	&#37;	Percent sign	
&	&#38;	Ampersand	&amp;
'	&#39;	Apostrophe	
(	&#40;	Left parenthesis	
)	&#41;	Right parenthesis	
*	&#42;	Asterisk	
+	&#43;	Plus sign	
,	&#44;	Comma	
-	&#45;	Hyphen	
.	&#46;	Period	
/	&#47;	Slash (solidus)	
:	&#58;	Colon	
;	&#59;	Semicolon	
<	&#60;	Less-than sign	&lt;

Character Symbol	Numeric Entity	Description	Character Entity
=	&#61;	Equal sign	
>	&#62;	Greater-than sign	&gt;
?	&#63;	Question mark	
@	&#64;	Commercial "At"	
[	&#91;	Left bracket	
\	&#92;	Backslash (reverse solidus)	
]	&#93;	Right bracket	
^	&#94;	Caret	
_	&#95;	Underline	
`	&#96;	Accent	
{	&#123;	Left curly bracket	
|	|	Bar	
}	&#125;	Right curly bracket	
~	&#126;	Tilde	
		Non-breaking space	
¡	&#161;	Inverted exclamation	
¢	&#162;	Cent sign	
£	&#163;	Pound sterling	
¤	&#164;	General currency sign	
¥	&#165;	Yen sign	
¦	&#166;	Broken vertical bar	
§	&#167;	Section sign	
¨	&#168;	Umlaut (dieresis)	
©	&#169;	Copyright	
ª	&#170;	Feminine ordinal	
«	&#171;	Left angle quote, guillemet left	
¬	&#172;	Not sign	
-	&#173;	Soft hyphen	
®	&#174;	Registered trademark	
¯	&#175;	Macron accent	
°	&#176;	Degree sign	
±	&#177;	Plus or minus	
2	&#178;	Superscript two	
3	&#179;	Superscript three	
´	&#180;	Acute accent	
µ	&#181;	Micro sign	
¶	&#182;	Paragraph sign	

Character Symbol	Numeric Entity	Description	Character Entity
·	&#183;	Middle dot	
,	&#184;	Cedilla	
¹	&#185;	Superscript one	
º	&#186;	Masculine ordinal	
»	&#187;	Right angle quote, guillemet right	
¼	&#188;	Fraction one-fourth	
½	&#189;	Fraction one-half	
¾	&#190;	Fraction three-fourths	
¿	&#191;	Inverted question mark	
À	&#192;	Capital A, grave accent	&Agrave
Á	&#193;	Capital A, acute accent	&Aacute;
Â	&#194;	Capital A, circumflex accent	&Acirc;
Ã	&#195;	Capital A, tilde	&Atilde;
Ä	&#196;	Capital A, dieresis or umlaut	&Auml;
Å	&#197;	Capital A, ring	&Aring;
Æ	&#198;	Capital AE diphthong (ligature)	&AElig;
Ç	&#199;	Capital C, cedilla	&Ccedil;
È	&#200;	Capital E, grave accent	&Egrave;
É	&#201;	Capital E, acute accent	&Eacute;
Ê	&#202;	Capital E, circumflex accent	&Ecirc;
Ë	&#203;	Capital E, dieresis or umlaut	&Euml;
Ì	&#204;	Capital I, grave accent	&Igrave;
Í	&#205;	Capital I, acute accent	&Iacute;
Î	&#206;	Capital I, circumflex accent	&Icirc;
Ï	&#207;	Capital I, dieresis or umlaut	&Iuml;
Ð	&#208;	Capital Eth, Icelandic	&ETH;
Ñ	&#209;	Capital N, tilde	&Ntilde;
Ò	&#210;	Capital O, grave accent	&Ograve;
Ó	&#211;	Capital O, acute accent	&Oacute;
Ô	&#212;	Capital O, circumflex accent	&Ocirc;
Õ	&#213;	Capital O, tilde	&Otilde;
Ö	&#214;	Capital O, dieresis or umlaut	&Ouml;
×	&#215;	Multiply sign	
Ø	&#216;	Capital O, slash	&Oslash;
Ù	&#217;	Capital U, grave accent	&Ugrave;
Ú	&#218;	Capital U, acute accent	&Uacute;
Û	&#219;	Capital U, circumflex accent	&Ucirc;

Character Symbol	Numeric Entity	Description	Character Entity
Ü	&#220;	Capital U, dieresis or umlaut	&Uuml;
Ý	&#221;	Capital Y, acute accent	&Yacute;
Þ	&#222;	Capital THORN, Icelandic	&THORN;
ß	&#223;	Small sharp s, German (sz ligature)	&szlig;
à	&#224;	Small a, grave accent	&agrave;
á	&#225;	Small a, acute accent	&aacute;
â	&#226;	Small a, circumflex accent	&acirc;
ã	&#227;	Small a, tilde	&atilde;
ä	&#228;	Small a, dieresis or umlaut	&auml;
å	&#229;	Small a, ring	&aring;
æ	&#230;	Small ae dipthong (ligature)	&aelig;
ç	&#231;	Small c, cedilla	&ccedil;
è	&#232;	Small e, grave accent	&egrave;
é	&#233;	Small e, acute accent	&eacute;
ê	&#234;	Small e, circumflex accent	&ecirc;
ë	&#235;	Small e, dieresis or umlaut	&euml;
ì	&#236;	Small i, grave accent	&igrave;
í	&#237;	Small i, acute accent	&iacute;
î	&#238;	Small i, circumflex accent	&icirc;
ï	&#239;	Small i, dieresis or umlaut	&iuml;
ð	&#240;	Small eth, Icelandic	&eth;
ñ	&#241;	Small n, tilde	&ntilde;
ò	&#242;	Small o, grave accent	&ograve;
ó	&#243;	Small o, acute accent	&oacute;
ô	&#244;	Small o, circumflex accent	&ocirc;
õ	&#245;	Small o, tilde	&otilde;
ö	&#246;	Small o, dieresis or umlaut	&ouml;
÷	&#247;	Division sign	
ø	&#248;	Small o, slash	&oslash;
ù	&#249;	Small u, grave accent	&ugrave;
ú	&#250;	Small u, acute accent	&uacute;
û	&#251;	Small u, circumflex accent	&ucirc;
ü	&#252;	Small u, dieresis or umlaut	&uuml;
ý	&#253;	Small y, acute accent	&yacute;
þ	&#254;	Small thorn, Icelandic	&thorn;
ÿ	&#255;	Small y, dieresis or umlaut	&yuml;

HOTDOG AND

NETSCAPE NAVIGATOR

HOTDOG WEB EDITOR

The HotDog Web Editor helps you design Web pages easily and efficiently. You can type HTML formatting tags directly, or you can select them from menus and pop-up lists. HotDog Web Editor is rated one of the best HTML authoring utilities currently available. Keep in mind that this software must be registered within 30 days of installation. For cost and registration information, check the HotDog Help menu or contact Sausage Software at `http://www.sausage.com`.

To install HotDog:
1. Create a `hotdog` directory on your hard disk (c:).
2. Copy `standard.exe` from the HotDog disk that comes with this book to `c:\hotdog`.
3. Open a DOS window, change to the `c:\hotdog` directory, and key in `c:\hotdog\standard.exe`.

To run HotDog:
1. Choose **Run** from the **File** menu (Windows 3.1) or the **Start** button (Windows 95) and key in `c:\hotdog\hotdog.exe`.

NETSCAPE NAVIGATOR

Netscape Navigator is one of the most popular Web browsers. It supports many interesting HTML 3.0 tags and gives you plenty of room for layout improvement. Netscape Navigator is currently available as shareware from the Netscape homepage: `http://home.netscape.com`. It also comes bundled with this book.

APPENDIX E

INTRODUCTION TO TABLES AND BACKGROUNDS

Tables are exciting, versatile tags featured in the not-yet-finalized HTML 3.0 standard. Using tables, you can achieve layout control previously impossible in HTML. For this reason, many savvy Web authors format the majority of their text using table elements.

Because tables are still evolving, this appendix will cover only the basic applications of the simpler table tags. You would be well advised to research tables on your own. HTML online resources in Appendix B contain a variety of excellent links which describe and teach tables. To view creative uses of tables, visit (among many others) Dave Siegel's Home Page, `http://www.best.com:80/~dsiegel/home.html` and Word `http://www.word.com/index.html`.

DEFINING THE BASIC STRUCTURE OF A TABLE

HTML tables are composed of rows (across) and columns (down) of cells. The contents of each cell can be formatted independently from the rest of the table. Rows and columns are delimited by borders. Borders can be visible or transparent and vary in width. The discussion that follows applies to Figure F.1, demonstrating two simple 2×2 tables.

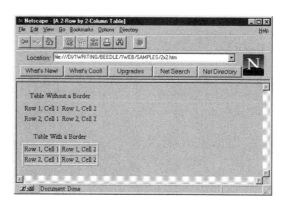

FIGURE F.1   A TWO-ROW BY TWO-COLUMN TABLE

The HTML for Figure F.1 is as follows:

```
<TABLE>
  <CAPTION>Table Without a Border</CAPTION>
  <TR>
    <TD>Row 1, Cell 1</TD>
    <TD>Row 1, Cell 2</TD>
  </TR>
  <TR>
    <TD>Row 2, Cell 1</TD>
    <TD>Row 2, Cell 2</TD>
  </TR>
</TABLE>
<BR>
<TABLE BORDER>
  <CAPTION>Table With a Border</CAPTION>
  <TR>
    <TD>Row 1, Cell 1</TD>
```

```
    <TD>Row 1, Cell 2</TD>
  </TR>
  <TR>
    <TD>Row 2, Cell 1</TD>
    <TD>Row 2, Cell 2</TD>
  </TR>
</TABLE>
```

- ⊘ Tables start and end with `<TABLE>`*table text*`</TABLE>` tags. The `BORDER` attribute specified in the second table renders the defining grid visible. Without `BORDER`, the grid remains transparent.

- ⊘ A Table title is defined with `<CAPTION>`...`</CAPTION>`. The caption is centered above the first row of the table.

- ⊘ A table row is defined with `<TR>`...`</TR>` tags.

- ⊘ Table cell data is defined with `<TD>`...`</TD>` tags. Notice that `<TD>` tag pairs must be fully nested inside a `<TR>` tag pair.

PRACTICE

Generate a simple 2-row × 3-column table with a visible border as follows:

Dan	Beer	$10000
Dorothy	Alfalfa	$25000

1. In the HTML editor, insert the following HTML:

```
<TABLE BORDER>
  <CAPTION><STRONG>Llamas for Sale</STRONG>
  </CAPTION>
  <TR>
    <TD>Dan</TD>
    <TD>Beer</TD>
    <TD>$10000</TD>
  </TR>
<TR>
    <TD>Dorothy</TD>
```

```
<TD>Alfalfa</TD>

<TD>$25000</TD>

</TABLE>
```

2. Save the document as `a:\table.htm`.

   In the browser, select **File, Open File** (or an equivalent command) to display table.htm. Your screen should resemble Figure F.2.

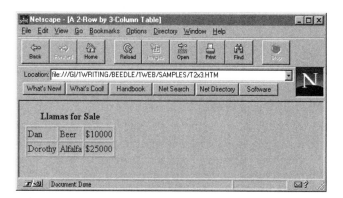

FIGURE F.2   A TWO-ROW BY THREE-COLUMN TABLE

FORMATTING BORDERS AND CELL CONTENTS

Border thickness can be customized. The proximity of the cell contents to the border can be specified, as can the formatting of cell contents themselves. The following examples illustrated these simple customizations.

BORDER WIDTH AND CELLSPACING

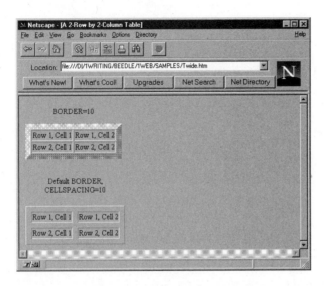

The HTML for Figure F.3 is as follows:

```
<TABLE BORDER=10>
  <CAPTION>BORDER=10</CAPTION>
  <TR>
    <TD>Row 1, Cell 1</TD>
    <TD>Row 1, Cell 2</TD>
  </TR>
  <TR>
    <TD>Row 2, Cell 1</TD>
    <TD>Row 2, Cell 2</TD>
  </TR>
```

```
</TABLE>

<BR>

<TABLE BORDER CELLSPACING=10>

  <CAPTION>Default BORDER, CELLSPACING=10
  </CAPTION>

  <TR>

    <TD>Row 1, Cell 1</TD>

    <TD>Row 1, Cell 2</TD>

  </TR>

  <TR>

    <TD>Row 2, Cell 1</TD>

    <TD>Row 2, Cell 2</TD>

  </TR>

</TABLE>
```

- Common `<TABLE>` attributes include BORDER, BORDER=*pixel width*, and CELLSPACING=*pixel width*.

- When BORDER is assigned any numeric value over one (BORDER=10), that value defines the pixel width of the table border and grid. BORDER without a numeric value defaults to a thin border width.

- The CELLSPACING attribute is a Netscape extension that defines the distance between the contents of each cell and the cell grid, often by making the border appear wide but transparent. The larger the number value assigned to CELLSPACING (CELLSPACING=10), the greater the distance between contents and border.

PRACTICE

Widen the border and add five-pixel cellspacing to the table in `table.htm`.

1. In the HTML editor, insert a five-pixel border and five-pixel cellspacing.

```
<TABLE BORDER=5 CELLSPACING=10>

  <TR>

  <TD>Dan</TD>

  <TD>Beer</TD>
```

```
    <TD>$10000</TD>
  </TR>


<TR>
  <TD>Dorothy</TD>
  <TD>Alfalfa</TD>
  <TD>$25000</TD>
</TABLE>
```

2. Save the document.

    In the browser, reload the file to display the updated `table.htm`. Your screen should resemble Figure F.4.

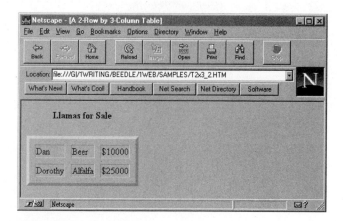

FIGURE F.4   TABLE BORDER=5; CELLSPACING=10

CELLPADDING AND COLUMN HEADINGS

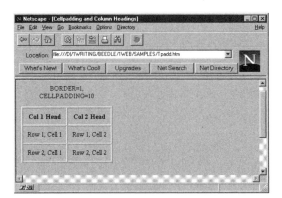

FIGURE F.5   A TABLE WITH CELLPADDING AND COLUMN HEADINGS

The HTML for Figure F.5 is as follows:

```
<TABLE BORDER CELLPADDING=10>

<CAPTION>BORDER=1 CELLPADDING=10</CAPTION>

<TR>

<TH>Col 1 Head</TH>

<TH>Col 2 Head</TH>

</TR>

.

.

.

</TABLE>
```

- The CELLPADDING attribute is a Netscape extension that defines the distance between the contents of each cell and the cell grid. The larger the number value assigned to CELLPADDING (CELLPADDING=10), the greater the distance between contents and border.

- A column heading is defined with <TH>...</TH> tags. These tags are always the first row <TR> of the table. Column headings are traditionally centered, often boldfaced at the top of the data column.

Add cellpadding and column headings to the table in `table.htm`.

1. In the HTML editor, insert a 10-pixel cellpadding value and enter column headings as follows.

```
<TABLE CELLPADDING=10>

  <TR>

    <TH>Name</TH>

    <TH>Feed</TH>

    <TH>Value</TH>

  </TR>
    .

    .

    .

  </TABLE>
```

2. Save the document.

3. In the browser, reload the file to display the updated `table.htm`. Your screen should resemble the following:

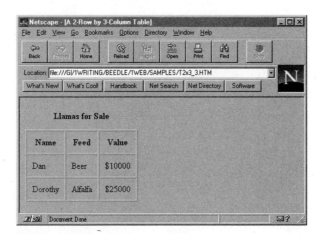

FIGURE F.6   CELLPADDING=10, COLUMN HEADINGS

CELL CONTENTS

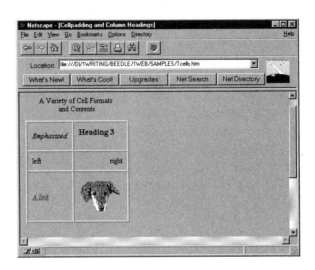

FIGURE F.7   FORMATTING CELL CONTENTS

The HTML for Figure F.7 is as follows:

```
<TABLE BORDER CELLPADDING=10>

  <CAPTION>A Variety of Cell Formats <BR>
  and Contents</CAPTION>

  <TR>

    <TD><EM>Emphasized</EM></TD>

    <TD><H3>Heading 3</H3></TD>

  </TR>

  <TR>

    <TD ALIGN="left">left</TD>

    <TD ALIGN="right">right</TD>

  </TR>

  <TR>

    <TD><A HREF="Tpadd.htm">A link</A></TD>
```

```
    <TD><IMG SRC="herman6.gif"></TD>
  </TR>

</TABLE>
```

◎ Each cell is a formatting domain all its own. Individual cells can contain all the standard formatting tags including headings, lists, links, paragraphs, and graphics.

◎ <TH>, <TR>, and <TD> cell alignment is addressed with ALIGN and VALIGN attributes. ALIGN=left|right|center controls horizontal positioning within the cell. VALIGN=top|middle|bottom controls vertical positioning within the cell.

◎ If a cell alignment attribute is inside <TR>, it applies to every cell in the row. If the attribute is inside <TH> or <TD>, it applies to the individual cell and will override an alignment attribute in <TR>.

PRACTICE

Add cell formatting to table.htm.

1. In the HTML editor, remove the border and change cell contents as follows.

```
<TABLE CELLPADDING=10>

  <CAPTION><STRONG>Llamas for Sale</STRONG>
  </CAPTION>

  <TR>

    <TH><EM>NAME</EM></TH>

    <TH><EM>FEED</EM></TH>

    <TH><EM>VALUE</EM></TH>

  <TH ALIGN="left"><EM>OWNERS</EM></TH>

  </TR>

  <TR>

    <TD><A HREF="dan.htm">Dan</A></TD>

    <TD>Beer</TD>

    <TD>$10000</TD>

    <TD>M/M Barrett</TD>

  </TR>

  <TR>
```

```
<TD><A HREF="dorothy.htm">Dorothy</A></TD>

<TD>Alfalfa</TD>

<TD>$25000</TD>

<TD>Col. G. P. Groves</TD>

  </TR>

</TABLE>
```

2. Save the document.
3. In the browser, reload the file to display the updated `table.htm`. Your screen should resemble Figure F.8.

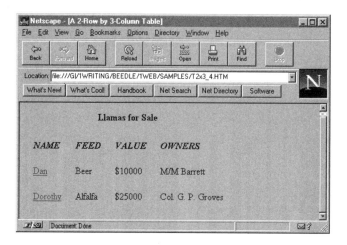

FIGURE F.8   SIMPLE CHANGES TO CELL FORMAT AND CONTENT

A SUMMARY ON BACKGROUNDS

A background can be an image tiled across the background of an HTML page, or it can be a solid color. Many browsers default to a dull gray background but you don't have to settle for it. By specifying a background graphic or color in your HTML, you have more control over the readability and impression of your Web page. Background graphics are defined inside the `<BODY>` tag as follows:

```
<BODY BACKGROUND="background filename">
```

Background colors are also defined inside the <BODY> tag as follows:

```
<BODY BGCOLOR="#$$$$$$">
```

where $$$$$$ is the hexadecimal value of Red, Green, and Blue (in that order). #FFFFFF is white; #000000 is black.

Along with BACKGROUND and BGCOLOR, you can also specify TEXT color, LINK color, visited (VLINK) link color, and active (ALINK) color. For example:

```
<BODY BACKGROUND="graphic.gif" BGCOLOR="#000000"
TEXT="#ffffff" LINK="#00ffff" VLINK="#ffff00"
ALINK="#ff0000">
```

The above example contains the hexadecimal equivalents for black, white, cyan, yellow, and red, respectively. The TEXT attribute defines the color of the text. For example, if the BGCOLOR is black you'll want your text to be a high contrast color such as white. The LINK attribute defines the color of links which haven't yet been clicked. The VLINK attribute defines the color of links which have already been clicked. The ALINK attribute defines the color of links which are currently being accessed. The active link color flashes when you click the link and the new document begins to download.

There are a variety of color lists available on the Web. One easy-to-use site is Rich Barrette's color page, http://www.ohiou.edu/~rbarrett/webaholics/ ver2/colors.html, or Infinet's color list http://www.infi.net/ wwwimages/colorindex.html.

HotDog makes it easy to assign background colors without needing the hexadecimal color equivalent. Simply select the **Format Document** command, then choose the Colors tab and select your colors from a visual palette.

Here are a few considerations about background images and colors:

- There can only be one background graphic or color per Web page.
- If the background image is a transparent GIF, the BGCOLOR color determines the color showing through the image.
- Backgrounds can be overridden by users. If the auto load image function is turned off, your background image won't display either.
- Keep background images very small. In Netscape, Web pages won't display properly until the background file has been completely downloaded.
- In general, white (light) backgrounds are best for text, and black backgrounds are best for photos.

GLOSSARY

ACRONYMS

ARPA	Advanced Research Projects Administration
ASCII	American Standard Code for Information Interchange
CERN	Centre European pour la Recherche Nucleaire
CGI	Common Gateway Interface
DoD	Department of Defense
DTD	Data Type Definition
GIF	Graphics Information File
HTML	Hypertext Markup Language
HTTP	Hypertext Transfer Protocol
JPG, JPEG	Joint Photographic Experts' Group
MIME	Multipurpose Internet Mail Extension
NCSA	National Center for Supercomputing Applications
NSF	National Science Foundation
SGML	Standardized General Markup Language
TIFF	Tagged Image File Format
URL	Uniform Resource Locator

TERMS

absolute address   Describes a complete pathname (often in a link) in reference to URLs. *Example:* `http://www.foo.com/directory/doc.html`.

address   On the Web, the electronic address used as an e-mail destination. *Example:* `joe@foo.edu`.

anchor   The HTML `<A>...</A>` tag that delineates a link to an outside resource. Also references a destination for an incoming link. *See* hypertext.

ASCII (American Standard Code for Information Interchange)   7-bit character code representing 128 characters.

attribute   In HTML, a property that modifies a start tag. Some attributes are mandatory; others are optional. *Examples:* `<IMG SRC="image.gif">` includes the mandatory attribute `SRC`, indicating that the following address is a `URL`; `<A NAME="text">` includes the optional attribute `NAME`, indicating that the following text serves as a link destination.

bandwidth   On the Web, refers to electronic carrying capacity. The greater the bandwidth, the faster the data transfer.

body   In HTML, the structure containing the bulk of the HTML document. Separate from the `HEAD`.

CERN (Centre European pour la Recherche Nucleaire)   The European Center for Particle Physics in Geneva, Switzerland, the birthplace of the World Wide Web.

CGI (Common Gateway Interface)   The specification on how browsers communicate with HTTP servers. Used with forms and other server queries.

character entity   In HTML, a string of text representing a special character or number. Always begins with an ampersand (`&`) and ends with a semicolon; *Examples:* `&lt;` is the character entity for the less-than symbol, `<`; `&#64;` is the @ symbol.

client   An end-user program that retrieves data from a server. On the Web, the browser is the client.

definition list   An HTML list structure `<DL>` that includes terms and definitions. Also known as a glossary list.

directory list   An HTML list structure, defined in HTML versions 1.0 and 2.0 but not 3.0. It creates a list of short paragraphs which are supposed to be formatted in columns.

domain   A nonnumeric name used to identify computers on the Internet. *Examples:* `www.foo.com`; `skycat.com`; and `www.bsd.uchicago.edu`.

element   Commonly describes the basic unit of HTML. Each tag is an element.

flame   To send or receive a hostile message. *Example:* "I got flamed."

form   HTML documents that solicit information from the enduser. Data is sent to the server, where responses can be generated based on user input.

GIF (Graphics Information File)   A commonly used graphic format on the Web.

helper programs   Utility programs that help browsers render specific kinds of data such as video or audio.

home page A type of Web page that serves as a starting point for Web travels. Also, the hierarchical head of a Web presentation. Home pages often include lists of hyperlinks.

hotlist In a browser, refers to a quick-reference list of favorite Web sites. Click and go.

HTTP (Hypertext Transfer Protocol) The Internet communication protocol used to transfer Web-formatted data between servers and clients.

hypertext The text or image on a Web page that, when clicked, links you to another Web resource or document. Also describes the system of presenting text and graphical information linked to other resources on the Web.

Hypertext Markup Language (HTML) The source code of every Web-formatted document. It is a subset of Standard Generalized Markup Language (SGML), a language for describing structured documents.

imagemap A clickable (active) graphic image. Typically, various regions of a graphic are designated as links to other parts of a Web site.

inline image An image that is automatically downloaded as part of the Web document text (unless the automatic download feature is disabled in the browser).

Internet A global network of networks that facilitates data exchange in a variety of formats.

JPG, JPEG (Joint Photographic Experts' Group) A commonly used graphic format on the Web. Used primarily with photographs.

link Hypertext that associates one HTML document to another. (The visible text or graphic is known as a "hotspot.") Also used in reference to anchor tags.

layout Describes elements that make up a Web-formatted document in terms of both structure and appearance (indentation values, font, and point size). *See* structure.

list element An item in an HTML list, designated by <LI>.

logical character format a.k.a. **soft format** The markup tags that suggest character styles. Visible formatting varies among browser software. *Examples:* strong emphasis <STRONG>, emphasis <EM>.

Lynx A character-based Web browser.

menu list An HTML list structure <ML>, defined in HTML versions 1.0 and 2.0 but not 3.0. It creates a list of short paragraphs.

MIME (Multipurpose Internet Mail Extension) A scheme that allows multimedia (text, sound, images, and video) to be included in e-mail.

nesting The practice of embedding elements inside other elements. In HTML, lists are frequently nested in other lists. Tags are often nested within other tags. *Example:* <P>This is <EM>important</EM>.</P>.

ordered list An HTML list structure `<OL>`, usually numbered.

Perl (Practical Extraction and Reporting Language) The language of choice for writing CGI scripts.

physical character format a.k.a. **hard format** The markup tags that dictate character styles. *Examples:* bold `<B>`, italic `<I>`.

platform Refers to the computer station's combined hardware and software. HTML is written to be platform-independent.

relative address Describes a pathname (often in a link) relative to the current document address. *Examples:* `directory/doc.html` is one directory in from the current directory; `doc.html` is in the current directory; `.../doc.html` is one directory up from the current directory.

server Refers to the networked computer than runs server software or to the software itself. Servers respond to client programs.

service provider An organization or business providing Internet access.

SGML (Standardized General Markup Language) The ISO standard describing markup languages. Facilitates platform-independent document transfer. HTML is a subset of SGML.

structure The elements that make up a Web-formatted document. These elements include paragraphs, six levels of headings, three types of lists, citations, addresses, four kinds of links, and much more. Structure dictates organizational hierarchy, not layout appearance. (Level 1 headings are higher up the ladder than level 2 and 3 headings, and so on). *See* layout.

tag In HTML, the typed text that describes HTML elements. Tags are enclosed in angle brackets. Empty tags contain no extra information, such as `<BR>` and `<HR>`. Container tags include supplied information such as `<IMG SRC="foo.html">`.

thumbnail A reduced version or portion of a larger graphic image.

TIFF (Tagged Image File Format) A graphics format you may encounter on the Web.

transparent image A GIF image whose background matches the background color of a Web document. This makes the image appear to "float" on the page.

Uniform Resource Locator (URL) The addressing scheme used to identify documents and resources on the Web. *Example:* `http://www.fedex.com`.

UNIX The most common operating system running Internet servers.

unordered list An HTML list structure `<UL>`, usually denoted with bullets or inline graphics.

INDEX